BINARY OPTIONS:

QUICK STARTERS GUIDE TO START BINARY OPTIONS TRADING

Andrew Johnson

© 2017

Sign Up & Join <u>Andrew Johnson's Mailing List!</u>

*EXCLUSIVE UPDATES

*FREE BOOKS

*NEW REALEASE ANNOUCEMENTS BEFORE ANYONE ELSE   GETS THEM

*DISCOUNTS

*GIVEAWAYS

FOR NOTIFACTIONS OF MY <u>*NEW RELEASES*</u> :

Never miss my next FREE PROMO, my next NEW RELEASE or a GIVEAWAY!

THIS BUNDLE INCLUDES THE FOLLOWING BOOKS:

A Beginner's Guide to Binary Options: Uncovering the Secrets of Binary Options

AND

Binary Options: The Ultimate Guide to Binary Options: Uncovering Binary Options Profit Making Secrets

AND

Binary Options: Strategies on How to Excel Trading Binary Options

TABLE OF CONTENTS

A Beginner's Guide to Binary Options: Uncovering the Secrets of Binary Options

Description

Uncover the secrets of binary options and start earning serious profits. *A Beginner's Guide to Binary Options* is your one-stop guide to everything that you need to know about trading binary options. It is a handy manual that will teach you what binary options are, how to trade binary options, the different strategies and the keys to success, as well as the common pitfalls which you should be aware of, and more.

INTRODUCTION

Congratulations on downloading this book and thank you for doing so.

The following chapters will discuss everything that you need to know about binary options. You will learn what binary options are, how to trade binary options, as well as the different strategies that you can use to rake in serious profits, and more.

There are plenty of books on this subject on the market, thanks for choosing this one! Every effort was made to ensure it is full of as much useful information as possible, please enjoy!

CHAPTER 1: UNDERSTANDING BINARY OPTIONS

Binary options are similar to forex and stock trading. However, instead of buying stocks or currencies, you merely speculate whether the price of a certain asset will rise or fall at a specified time. Its simplicity is one of the things that draw many investors to binary options. You do not even have to purchase any stock or asset; you only have to wager whether the current price of a certain asset will increase or decrease at the expiry time. Binary options are an option contract that has a fixed risk and fixed payout.

Trading binary options vs. gambling

There are similarities between trading binary options and gambling. In fact, in some jurisdictions, trading binary options are considered a form of gambling. Like a game of baccarat where you can choose whether the winning hand is either the banker or the player, binary options let you place a wager whether the price of an asset will increase (Call) or decrease (Put) at the expiry time. Similar to gambling, there is also a predetermined payout each time you get the correct outcome.

So, is trading binary options considered gambling? It depends. If you trade binary options using mere guesswork and the success of every trade that you make relies solely on pure luck, then you are gambling. However, if you view your every wager as an investment decision and take the time and effort to research the market, as well as the different assets that are being traded, then you may be considered an investor or trader, and not a mere gambler. Take note, however, that being a gambler is not a completely bad thing, especially once you see how the high rollers dominate the baccarat table.

In the end, whether trading binary options makes you an investor/trader or a gambler does not matter. What matters is how much profit you have made, if any.

Binary options vs. forex and stock trading

Unlike forex and stock trading where you need to purchase currencies or stocks and sell them when their price increases, you do not have to purchase any trading asset when you engage in binary options. You only have to speculate whether the value of an asset will be higher or lower than its current price at the expiry date of the trade. Also, when you trade stocks or currencies, you have no idea how much you can profit in the future. In fact, some stocks that you buy today may not even make any income for you in the future even if you sell them. This is true especially when the value of your stocks drops significantly. In binary options, you will already know the fixed amount that you can earn even before you commence a trade.

When trading stocks or currencies, you will usually have to wait for weeks, months, or even a year, just to see a significant change in value. In binary options, you can double your investment in less than a day's time. In fact, you can do it even within an hour.

Another difference is that you do not have to worry about surcharges, volume restrictions and fees, and other charges when you trade binary options.

The Basics

Trading binary options is easy. No matter which platform you use, there are two main options that you need to know:

Call

You should choose the Call option if you think that the value of an asset will be above its current price at the expiry time.

Put

You should choose the Put option if you think that the value of an asset will be lower than its current price at the expiry time.

Depending on the trading platform that you use, Call/Put option may also be referred to as Above/Below, Up/Down, High/Low, Rise/Fall, and others. It does not matter what nomenclature is used. The trade remains the same. What matters is that you pick the right option (Call or Put), and the value of the underlying stock must match your choice at the end of the trading period.

Strike price

A strike price simply refers to the value at which an underlying asset may be bought or sold at a specified time. When trading binary options, a strike price can be a Call or a Put. For a Call option, the strike price represents the price at which the asset can be bought at a specified time. For a Put option, the strike price signifies the price at which an underlying asset may be sold.

Expiry time

The expiry time refers to the end of a trading period. It is the time when you can determine if you have chosen the right option (Call or Put) and the outcome is revealed.

In-the-money vs. out-the-money

On the one hand, in-the-money means that you made the right wager. It is a winning position. It means that you have earned a profit. On the other hand, out-the-money is the opposite. It means that you have lost your money in the trade.

Long-term option

This option simply means that the trade will last for a longer duration of time. In binary options, a long-term may refer to a single trading session that lasts for one whole day (24 hours) up to several weeks, though some even last longer than a month.

Speed option

The speed option is one that is similar to casino gambling because the outcome is revealed in just a few seconds. Speed option trading can be as fast as 30 seconds, 1 minute, or even up to 5 minutes. Of course, you may also encounter different trading periods depending on the platform that you are using.

One touch option

With one touch option, you need to be able to determine if the value of an asset will exceed a certain level during a trading period. Take note that the value of the asset does not have to maintain such level until the expiry date. All that is needed is for the price of the underlying asset to exceed a certain level during the trading session, whether before or at the expiry time. If you want to earn up to 500%, then this is the way to go. However, this option is not recommended for beginners. You first need to acquire adequate knowledge and skills to handle this option with competence.

Pairs option

Unlike other options, this includes wagering on "pairs," for example, gold and silver. You need to determine whether one asset will outperform the other within a specified period of time.

Assets

Assets are financial instruments that have value. When trading binary options, you do not have to buy the assets, you simply have to speculate whether their value will rise or fall.

When trading binary options, there are a number of underlying assets that you can choose from: stocks, indexes, commodities, and currency pairs.

Stocks

When trading binary options, it would be helpful if you get yourself acquainted with the performance of various international stocks. But do not worry; the process is still simple. You do not have to purchase any stock. You simply have to determine if the price of a certain stock willrise or fall.

Index

This refers to a group of companies that share the same market sector or stocks that have commonalities. If a company or several companies belonging to the same index perform excellently during a period, then it will have a positive impact upon their index representation. This usually results in an increase in the value of assets, which is a golden opportunity for binary options traders.

Commodities

When you engage in binary options trading, you will see different kinds of commodities, such as gold, silver, oil, and sugar, among many others. Still, you do not need to buy any commodity, you only have to speculate whether a price of a certain commodity will increase or decrease at the expiry date.

There are many factors that affect the prices of commodities; therefore, they are harder to predict. If you are a beginner, you should first gain more experience before you deal with commodities.

Currency pairs

There are various currency pairs that you will find when you visit a trading platform. The most common that you will find is EUR/USD. This is the way to trade forex using binary options. The process remains the same. You simply have to determine whether the exchange rate will increase or decrease. The first currency is referred to as the base currency, while the second currency is known as the quote currency.

Bear market vs. bull market

These are terms that are used to describe the status of a market. On the one hand, a bear market signifies a quite negative sentiment, because it means that the prices of certain underlying assets are decreasing or about to drop. On the other hand, a bull market means that the prices of certain underlying assets are increasing or about to increase.

So, is a bear market bad for you? Answer: No. Take note that in binary options, you do not purchase any asset. This is one of the benefits of trading binary options. It has a dual nature. You can make a profit even if the price of certain assets decreases.

It is important to know if the market is a bear or a bull market so that you will know where to place your wager. If it is a bull market, then you should make a Call; however, if it is a bear market, you should take the Put option.

Brokers and trading platforms

An important thing to do before you start investing in binary options is to identify the best brokers and trading platforms that you can use. You can easily find many brokers by making a search online. However, you need to choose the one that is reliable, trustworthy, and best suits your needs.

Here is a list of well-established binary options brokers. Take note that even popular trading platforms may change their management team; therefore, what may be considered the best brokers today may no longer be considered highly recommended tomorrow. Be sure to check the latest rating and reviews given by previous buyers.

- iq option (www.iqoption.com)

- 24option (www.24option.com)

- Finpari (www.finpari.com)

- OptionRobot (www.optionrobot.com)

- Automated Binary (www.automatedbinary.com)

- fortuneJack (www.fortunejack.com) *bitcoin casino with binary options*

Before you sign up for an account, be sure to check the minimum deposit that is required. Also take note of the banking methods, such as the available options for making a deposit and for withdrawal. This is important because it is not uncommon to see platforms that accept many ways to deposit money to fund your account, but only has limited options for making a withdrawal. You would not want to be happy about your high profits only to have issues with withdrawing your money. After all, all profits are merely as good as numbers on the screen unless you are able to withdraw them into real cash. Many brokers will also require you to submit documents for identification purposes before you are able to withdraw your money. Make sure you know exactly what these documents are and that you have them in your possession before making a deposit. If the specific documents are not clearly stated on the website, do not hesitate to contact customer support.

Sadly, it is very easy to make a deposit, but there can be many issues when it comes to withdrawing your money. This is another reason why you should only use a reliable platform with a trustworthy broker.

What to look for in a binary options broker

Some brokers come and go, while others remain. It is important for you to know what to look for in a broker, and you must work with a broker that best suit your needs. Here are some important things to take note of:

Capitalization

Does your broker have enough capital to continue in business for a long term? The danger with a broker that does not have enough funds is the high probability of going bankrupt.

When a broker goes bankrupt, you can no longer recover your deposited funds, any pending wagers, or profits. Therefore, it is important that your broker has enough capital to continue in business.

Regulation

Is your broker regulated by the government or an independent third party? Does it have a license to operate? To lower the probability of getting scammed, you should work with a licensed broker. Many brokers are regulated by CySEC, which is a member of the European Union. In the U.S., the Commodity Futures and Trading Commission (CFTC) functions as a regulatory body.

Payout

The payout is very important. Take note of how much can you earn for a speed option and for a long-term trade. Remember that the fixed payout in binary options is already known even before you place a wager. Of course, the higher is the payout, the better.

Customer support

How many ways can you contact the customer support team? And how long does it take for the customer support to respond? A good way to find out is by sending a message to their customer support. Simply inquire about something, and see how quickly and well the support team can handle your concern. Also check if the site offers a live chat support feature or if there is a number that you can call anytime.

Trading platform

Of course, one of the most important things to consider is how you feel about using the trading platform. Does it look nice to you? Are you satisfied with its trading tools which can help you come up with a better investment decision? It is not only the design or layout but also the features which the platform offers that must be considered.

Mobile trading

It is a plus if you can access your account and make a wager with your mobile phone. These days, a mobile feature is common.

However, if you do not intend to use your phone for making a trade, then this would not be a concern.

Demo account

If you are just a beginner, you will find having a demo account useful. Most brokers offer a free demo account. A demo account will allow you to trade in real time and test your strategy without wagering real money. In case a broker you really like does not offer a demo account, you can still use the same broker. Simply register an account with another site that has a demo account. You can use your favorite broker for the account with real money and use the other site solely for the demo account.

Popularity and reviews

How popular is the site? Does it appear in search engines' page results, and is it mentioned in several articles on binary trading? Also, be sure to check the reviews written by other investors. Be cautious of dealing with brokers, even with reputable brokers. There are some brokers that start nicely but become corrupt after some time. Also, not all articles that you read online that promote a certain broker can be trusted. As part of online marketing, many brokers hire freelance writers to write something positive about them.

Number of available assets

Find out the underlying assets that the platform supports, as well as how many options you have. If you are into currency trading, then the platform must offer multiple currencies. If a broker only offers a few currencies, then it is a signal that the broker might not be completely serious about what it is doing.

Banking options

As already mentioned, you should check the available methods for making a deposit, as well as for a withdrawal. Take note of the minimum and maximum amounts that can be deposited and withdrawn. It is also important to know how long it will take you to receive your money in case of a withdrawal.

Security

The platform must have a secured trading environment. Is the site encrypted or not? You must be confident that you can safely leave your money in your account. Be sure that all financial transactions are secured and encrypted.

CHAPTER 2: RISKS AND BENEFITS

Before you step into the world of binary trading, you should know the risks and benefits that you will be facing. Like any other business venture, trading binary options have certain risks that can cause you to lose all of your investment; however, it also has a number of notable benefits that counterbalance the risks associated with binary options.

The risks

Market risk

Just like other investments, there is an overall market risk involved when trading binary options. Although there are ways on how to predict how the market will move, there is no well-established method that can guarantee toward which direction the market will take.

Lack of ownership

Unlike trading stocks or currencies, you do not buy any asset when you engage in binary options. The only thing you have is your funds which you will use to place a wager on whether the value of an underlying asset will rise or fall at the expiry date. Therefore, you do not exercise any ownership over any stock, currency, or asset.

No liquidity

Binary options do not have liquidity. Once you enter into a trade, you have to wait for the trading session or period to end. During such time, there is nothing you can do but wait and hope for the best. Although there are platforms that will allow you to cancel a trade, you can only do so within a limited and short timeframe, and you will have to pay a fee for it. Usually, traders cancel a trade not to exercise any liquidity, but merely to cancel a trade that was erroneously made. For example, instead of choosing Call, you mistakenly select Put. If liquidity is very important to you, binary options may not be a good choice. However, take note that liquidity should not be a serious issue with binary options, because the trading period usually does not last long, and you can choose just how fast you want your trades to be completed, which can be as quick as less than a minute.

High-risk investment

Although binary options offer a high-profit potential, the risk involved is also high, if not higher. When you're in-the-money, the profit depends on the payout, which may be around 90% or less. However, if you lose the trade, you will not be able to save or get anything back from what you invested in that particular trade. Meaning, if you wager $100, you lose the whole $100 instantly. Unlike in trading stocks or forex, you can continue to hold possession of the stocks and sell them once their value increases. But, of course, it is difficult to get a 90% profit return in stocks and forex, and it will take a lot of time.

Limited opportunity

Unlike in trading stocks or forex, if you get lucky, the value of certain stocks or currency can increase by 200% or even more. In binary options, how much you will earn is already revealed before you even place a wager. If you think about it, this is not really a big disadvantage. In fact, many investors prefer to know the highest profit they can earn before they even place an investment. The only real difference here is that in binary options there is no way to get more than the stipulated payout. Of course, you can always initiate another trade to earn more.

Losing is normal

The normal trend in binary options is this: Majority of the people who invest in binary options lose their money. This, unfortunately, is the sad fact of binary options trading. You might hear or read about some investors who quickly triple their investment in less than a week's time, but there are more stories where investments turn into zero in less than a day of active trading.

Is it for you?

If your entrepreneurial spirit is not crushed by the number of risks associated with binary options, then it is time for you to find out the wonderful benefits that binary options offer.

The benefits

Simplicity

The beautiful simplicity of binary trading is one of the things that makes it very attractive. Even if you do not have any gambling or trading experience, you can easily learn how to trade binary options in less than 5 minutes. After all, you can just always pick between Call and Put. But, of course, if you want to increase your chances of making a profit or if you want to have a regular stream of income, you need to exert serious and continued effort, study, patience, and practice.

High return

If you think that a 30% increase in stocks is already something to be proud of, wait until you see how much you can make with binary options. When trading binary options, a single trade can quickly give you a 190% return – or even higher (your original investment + the profit) - within a short period of time.

Fixed payout

When trading binary options, you will already be shown a fixed profit that you will earn in the case of a favorable outcome. This is unlike other investments where you do not know how much money you can make. Also, the payout in binary options is usually high.

Quick turnover rate

One of the impressive things about trading binary options is its fast turnover rate. You can use the speed option and complete a trade in less than a minute. In other forms of investment, you will have to wait weeks, and even months, just to profit a little.

Asset variety

With binary options, you will have a lot of choices as to where to put an investment. After all, you would not purchase any stock or asset. In fact, some brokers will allow you to trade with a minimum amount of $1. If you use bitcoins, you can even find brokers that will allow you to trade binary options for less than a dollar per trade.

Gambling factor

Let us accept the truth that gambling is fun. This is why many people get addicted to it. Now, when you become a professional trader, there is always a part of the business where you can feel that gambling factor.

After all, there is no 100% guarantee that your trades will always be in-the-money. Of course, this does not mean that you should just gamble and rely on pure luck. You should always do your research, study the market and the underlying assets, come up with a strategy, place a wager, and hope for the best.

Controlled risk

Trading binary options is simple, and everything is made clear. There are no hidden charges or surcharges. The amount that you invest in a particular trade is also the exact amount that you risk. Therefore, if you only want to risk a thousand dollars, then just fund your account with the said amount and you would not have to worry about anything else.

Instant trading

Many brokers have trading platforms that will allow you to trade binary options using your mobile phone. Therefore, you would not have to worry about using a desktop computer just to manage your account or make a trade. By simply using your mobile phone, you can log into your account and commence trading anytime, anywhere.

CHAPTER 3: STRATEGIES

Applying the right strategies at the right time is crucial to success. Despite the unstable market and the tough odds, strategies will make it possible for you to have a steady stream of profits, provided you know how and when to use them. However, unlike a casino game where you simply need to adjust the amount of your wager and play with the possible choices, success in trading binary options demands more diligent study, research, and analysis.

Fundamental analysis

Considered as the lifeblood of investment, fundamental analysis is something that you need to learn if you want to increase the probability of making a profit. You need to analyze the economy and the surrounding factors which affect the economy, such as the news, financial statements of businesses, etc. For example, in the case where a high employment rate has been announced in the U.S., you can expect that the value of USD will increase. Take note, however, that one factor alone is not enough. You must also consider other things that influence the economy which, in turn, will have an impact on various underlying assets. Also, do not underestimate the speeches and messages released by organizations and publicized by the media. These things can significantly influence market behavior, which can strongly affect the prices of many kinds of assets.

Fundamental analysis is not just about the economy. Of course, one of the major forces that drive the economy is business. Therefore, you need to take a closer look and study various businesses, as well as how they affect one another. You have to analyze their financial statements, their competitors, and their performance in the market.

Technical analysis

This type of analysis is where you analyze the past performance of an underlying asset in order to gauge its future movement. Different tools and indicators are usually used, such as graphs, charts, and others.

If you do not like numbers, then technical analysis is the way to go. The most common charts used when one does a technical analysis are the line and candlestick charts.

Algorithmic and signals

This is where you rely on computers and applications to show the best options to invest your money in. The application can be installed on your computer and it will do the analysis for you. Although this sounds easy and amazing, this is not a highly recommended method to use. On the one hand, no computer program or application has yet been invented that can always read the movement of a living market. On the other hand, it is good to use this method to quickly gain additional information.

Co-integration trading

This strategy relies on the strong correlation between two underlying assets. This usually happens when two assets belong to the same industry or share the same market. Due to the high correlation, you may find that their prices are almost always close to each other. Therefore, when there is a significant gap between the prices of the two assets, you can assume that it has occurred because one of them has become weak. However, such gap is only for a temporary period. Due to their high correlation, their prices will again be somewhat close. Therefore, you are now one step ahead. The only thing left for you to determine now is whether to place a Call on the stock whose price has dropped or a Put on the stock with a higher price.

Reading charts and graphs

Charts and graphs are the main tools of binary options traders. They are used to be able to read trends and predict the future movement of underlying assets. Charts also show just how volatile certain assets are. When an asset clearly shows an up-and-down trend, then it is more volatile than an asset with a relatively smooth movement. Be it noted, however, that trends change.

Reading a chart may seem easy, but predicting where the next movement will be can be very tricky. Most traders will rely on patterns and do short-term trades. The problem with patterns is that although they exist, they are not always present. Worse, patterns change, just as trends also change.

When you see and confirm that a pattern is in play, you need to be able to decide and place your wager quickly. Patterns do not last very long and the market does not cease to move. Also, if you do not recognize any pattern, do not make up a pattern. If you do not see one, then admit that there is nothing and just try again some other time. Unfortunately, just for the purpose of commencing a trade, many traders force to see a pattern even when no pattern is actually present. When this happens, your investment decision will only be as good as a mere guesswork, and you will be at a high risk of losing your investment.

Line chart

A line chart is the most common kind of chart used not only in trading binary options but also in other investments. It is a financial tool that can help you make a better investment decision.

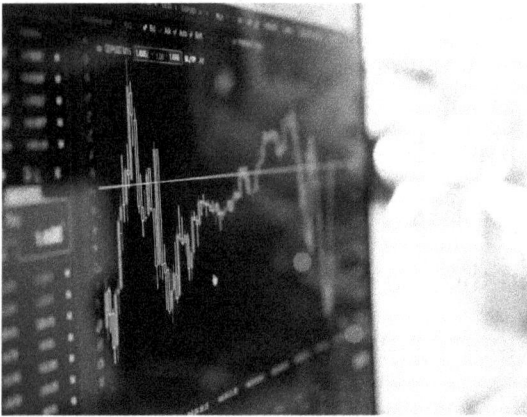

A line chart is formed by connecting with a line the past values or prices of a certain asset over a given timeframe. Therefore, it can clearly show you the price movements and the prevailing trend.

Candlestick chart

The candlestick chart reveals more information than a line chart. So, if you want to do more analysis, you have to learn how to utilize the candlestick chart. This chart shows the market's open and close, high and low. Each candlestick has a body which signifies a range between the opening and closing of a day's trade. When you look at a candlestick chart and see the body of the candle filled in, it means that the price of an asset at closing was lower than it was at the time of opening. If empty, then it means that it was higher.

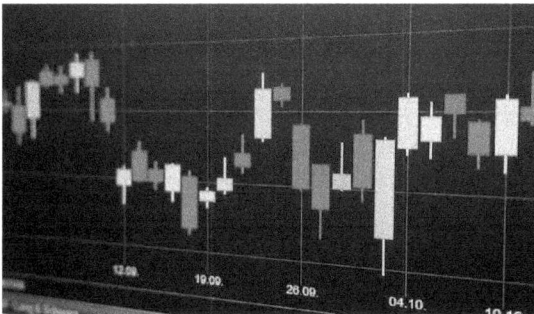

The slim lines that you can see below and above the body are referred to as shadows. The shadows represent the high and low prices of a day's trade. If the body of a candlestick is filled in but the upper shadow is short, it means that the opening price of an asset for that day was closer to its value for the previous day. If the body of the candlestick is not filled in and the upper shadow is short, it simply means that the close for the day's trade was near the high. Candlesticks may be confusing for beginners, but they can also be helpful in making an investment decision.

Trading time frame

Proper timing is essential in trading binary options. Therefore, understanding the time frame that you should use is also important. You will find many time frames to choose from. A trading session can be as fast as a minute, or even less, but it can also take weeks or even a month. Usually, the longer the time frame is, the higher will be the payout.

If you are into gambling then a time frame of 2 minutes, 1 minute, or 30 seconds would be the one for you. However, the problem with this time frame is that it is very hard to predict. Even when you do research, it may not be enough considering that time also moves as you do the research. This time frame is just too short and usually offers the lowest payout of around 70%, depending on the platform that you are using.

The time frame that is commonly used by traders is around 10-15 minutes per trade. However, since this is still a short-term period, this is only good if you base your decisions on your quick analysis of the graphs and charts. If you are into technical analysis, then this is a good option. This option also offers a higher payout.

Time frames ranging from 30 minutes to 24 hours or more are good to use if you are into fundamental analysis. Of course, you can always add technical analysis to your research. Considering the difficulty of predicting the outcome of such long time frame, this option offers the highest payout. Depending on your preference, 30 minutes may still be considered a short period, but you can always choose a time frame that will best suit your needs. A trade can last for as long as a day, a week, and sometimes even longer. Despite the numerous trading options, professional traders usually stick to time frames that are just less than an hour long, subject to exceptions.

Conservative betting

Conservative betting is when you wager only a small percentage of your total funds, preferably around 1%-2%. This will ensure that you can enjoy more trades and stay in the game longer. Conservative betting is a good strategy if you have a high success rate. Although you earn a lower amount than aggressive betting, your high volume of successful trades can easily pile up and be a big amount. If you are a beginner, stick to conservative betting.

Aggressive betting

Aggressive betting is when you wager a big percentage of your total funds; for example, betting at least 10% of your funds. Of course, the most aggressive style is to simply wager your whole funds in a single trade. By betting aggressively, you can earn more profit within a short period of time; however, you can also lose all your investment quickly. Only use this kind of betting strategy if you are highly confident of the outcome of a particular trade. Of course, the most aggressive way of betting is by going all in each time you enter a trade.

Double down

Double down is essentially doubling your bet each time you lose a wager, also known as the Martingale system. This betting strategy is very aggressive and is used by many gamblers. So, how does it work?

Each time you lose a wager, you simply double your bet until you go in-the-money (win a wager). For example, you wager $30 (or lower). If you lose, your next wager will be $60. If you lose again, your next bet will be $120, then $240, $480, $960, and so on. What it does is that once you get even a single win, you always get a profit equal to the amount of your first wager. However, trading binary options does not work like the casino. The payout that you will receive will be less than 100% of your wager. The amount of the payout depends on the broker, so be sure to get a broker that offers the highest payout. A payout of around 90% is good. You might want to increase your wager a bit more to cover for the missing 10%. However, just to avoid any complicated computations, you can simply double your bet each time you lose a wager. Once you go in-the-money, you go back to the $30 bet (or lower) and start over.

At first glance, this betting strategy looks promising. However, the fact is that countless gamblers and binary options traders have lost money because of this strategy. Unfortunately, when you do a good number oftrades based on mere guesswork or insufficient research, it is not surprisingto encounter 10 out-the-money outcomes in a row. In fact, you can get even more than 20 out-the-money outcomes in succession. The Martingale is an aggressive style of betting. Just imagine how much money you would have lost when you reach the 10th or even just the 5th wager. Your losses also continue to double and pile up. If you had an infinite amount of money to invest, then this is a good strategy. However, nobody has an infinite amount of money. Moreover, similar to a casino, there is also a maximum wager or ceiling to be observed when you trade binary options, the amount of which depends on the platform that you use. There is a limit as to how many times you can double your wager. The maximum wager may be around a thousand dollars up to $20,000, or even higher. Note: Do not use this strategy for a long period of time.

Flat betting

Flat betting is considered a conservative betting strategy, provided you do not wager a huge percent of your funds. Ideally, you can wager 1%-2% of your total funds for each bet that you make. It is called flat betting because unlike the Martingale strategy, you do not increase your wager. Whether you go in-the-money or out-the-money, you just stick to the same wager. This is a good strategy to use when you have a high success rate.

Follow the trend

This is a very common strategy used even by those who have not read anything about binary options. Therefore, be cautious of using this strategy. As the name already implies, it means that you simply have to follow the trend. You should use this with the speed option, so you would not miss the trend. Do not just follow any increase or decrease in value of an underlying asset. Instead, analyze the graph and try to look for a pattern. The pattern can be the trend that you are looking for.

Corrective

This strategy can be applied when you notice a sudden surge in price, either a dramatic increase or decrease. This price spike is only brief and temporary. Soon, the price will balance by reverting back to its value just before the spike, or at least somewhere close to it. When you see this kind of trend, then you are one step ahead.

Breakout

This applies when you deal with currency pairs. When a currency pair observes a tight price range for a long period of time, if you see them break out, there is a high chance that the breakout of the price range will continue, and it will take some time before they can regain their normal price range.

5-minute strategy

This is a strategy that many beginners use. The method is simple: Look for an asset that has a stable movement and simply follow the trend. Just balance the graph. For example, after a bad drop in price, bet on a Call, and vice versa. This, in fact, can also be applied to any speed option, including trades as fast as 30 seconds.

Mixed

A good way to trade binary options is not to stick to a single strategy. This is because the market itself does not follow the same behavior, and it does not react the same way. A suggested method is to use one strategy for the first trade, then use a different strategy for the next trade, then another for the third trade, and so on. Once you run out of good strategies, you go back to your first strategy and start over. Of course, if circumstances strongly show that a different strategy should be applied, then be flexible enough to do so. This approach is not advisable for beginners. However, after a week or two of active trading, then you can also apply this strategy.

Asset mastery

Pick an asset. It can be a single one or several. One asset would be enough. What you will do is to find out everything that you can about your chosen asset. You should follow it on the news and get regular updates regarding that asset every day, if possible. It will be your asset. By fully marking or embracing an asset like this, you will be able to gain a better foresight. Therefore, you will be able to give a better prediction and your success rate will increase. Once you are satisfied with your success rate on a single asset, add another, then another. The more assets that you can master, the better. Mastery of an asset also means having an understanding of the different factors that can affect its value.

Beware of the gambler's fallacy

Most people think that in a game of odds, when a certain event happens many times, it will happen less in the future. For example, when you flip a coin thrice and you get heads three times, there is a higher probability that the next coin flip will be tails. After all, in 50-50 odds like a coin flip, getting four heads in succession is unusual. This is the gambler's fallacy.

The thing is, before you flip the coin, the odds of getting heads and tails are equal: 50% for heads and 50% for tails — and the odds remain the same right after you flip the coin. Therefore, even after getting three heads in a row, the probability of getting another heads on the fourth coin flip is also 50-50. Meaning, even though you get three heads in a row, there is still a 50% probability that the next coin flip will be heads, just as there is a 50% probability that it can be tails.

How is this related to trading binary options? Well, some see binary options like a flip of a coin or anything that has 50-50 odds. They think that if Call has won many times in succession, the next winning option regardless of what asset you place your wager on should be a Put.

You should understand that the outcome of a trade does not depend upon another trade. Even if Put wins twenty times, it does not mean that Call will have a greater chance of winning on the next wager. This is only if you base your decision on mere 50-50 odds. The best way is still to work and exert effort: Do your market research and study the assets and their values.

Take note that binary options do not depend on random generator machines; they are not run by robots. The factors that influence the prices of the assets come from real people and real businesses. Also, the assets do not have a memory of their own.

It is also worth noting that trading binary options is not like a mere coin flip with 50-50 odds. In fact, this is what makes it a good investment, because there are factors that you can consider which can reveal the outcome of a trade. You can make the odds work in your favor.

CHAPTER 4: KEYS TO SUCCESS

Whether you want to trade binary options for fun or for serious profit, you should know the best practices, so you can increase your chances of success. And, since there is nothing fun about losing money, you might as well aim to make a profit. Here are the keys that will help you succeed.

Money management

Even if you get a regular stream of profits, you may find yourself bankrupt in the future if you do not manage your money properly. Money management does not only refer to the money that you use to trade binary options, but how you manage all the money that you have. Do not invest in binary options the money that you need to pay for your electric bill and other obligations. One important thing to decide upon is how much money you are going to invest in binary options. Be sure to invest only the money that you can afford to lose.

You should also decide on how much money are you going to invest per trade. This, of course, also depends upon your betting strategy. For beginners, it is strongly suggested that you stick to conservative betting.

Cash out

This is also a part of money management. In fact, this is a very important part. You will often find many traders who feel happy about their successive profits. They get to double or even triple their investment every day; then after a week, they lose everything. The idea behind accumulating all your profits is to have morefunds so that you can increase the amount of your wager. However, many traders forget to withdraw or cash out, even just a part of the profits. Cashing out will help you minimize your losses.

It is not surprising that even the best strategy will also experience some losses. Therefore, you need to cash out to save a part of your funds. For example, you get successful trades for the first 9 days, with a profit of just 15% daily. Then on the 10thday you get very unlucky and lose everything. Had you cashed out your profits, you would have a positive profit despite losing your funds on the 10th day.

Another very important thing about cashing out is this: it is the only way that you really enjoy your profit. Why? Because as long as you do not cash out and turn those profits into real cash, they are only as good as free virtual demo funds.

Meaning, they are just numbers on the screen and nothing more. It is the very act of cashing out that turns them into a real profit.

You do not have to withdraw all your funds or all your profits. If you really want to grow your funds, you can just withdraw about 10%-20% of your profits. This depends on your preference, but be sure to have a plan on how and when do you intend to make a withdrawal. The sad truth is that many traders lose their money before they even think about clicking that withdraw option.

Research and analysis

By now, you should already know the importance of doing a research and analysis of the market and the underlying assets. This is your advantage, your edge against the tough odds. Therefore, you need to research well. When you analyze the trends or the data that you have, you need to let go of personal preferences and prejudices.

The market does not care about what you think or how you feel. Be smart and objective. And above all, be practical and reasonable. If only you can look closely, you will see that the market movement is actually reasonable, if you know all the right facts and can analyze them correctly.

Focus on the assets

The graphs and the charts make the act of trading binary options look so sophisticated. Those small numbers on the screen, those moving lines and stark colors, these are the things you want to see. They make you think that you truly understand how to trade just by looking at them. But, no — such is not enough. When you trade binary options, you need to focus on the underlying assets themselves, as well as the businesses. Although you can find some patterns when you just rely on graphs, such is not enough. After all, these patterns do not always happen. And many times, the patterns are impossible to notice in the beginning. And even if you see them, there is no assurance that the trend will not change.

Focus on the assets. Research and study the assets that you are interested in. Read the news about them and look at the financial statements of their companies, as well as related businesses.

Focus on the numbers

It is easy to make something look attractive, especially these days when you can instantly spread a message to the whole world with just a click of a mouse. Although you are expected to read and follow on the latest updates regarding the economy, business, and other factors that may affect the prices of certain underlying assets, you should not believe everything at once.

Always take everything that you read or hear with a grain of salt. Unfortunately, words can easily be twisted. They are subject to various interpretations and can even serve both contradicting views at the same time. However, numbers cannot lie. Even if one company promotes its stocks to be doing really well, you will know that it is a lie by looking at the numbers. Although numbers can also be manipulated, they are much harder to manipulate than words; and numbers cannot lie.

Do not chase after your losses

Losses are bound to happen. There are trades that will simply not give you any return. But, never chase after your losses. It will only make you trade under pressure, and it will also make the probability of losing more money even higher.

Instead of chasing after your losses, you should chase after more profits. There are many ways to chase after your losses. The most common, of course, is by increasing the amount of your wager. The problem with this is that your current strategy may not be fit for an aggressive style of betting. Another major problem with this is that your funds may not be ready for such a high bet amount. Although there is a higher payout potential, this is also an effective way to quickly lose all of your investment.

The importance of keeping a journal

A journal is not a must to have but it is highly recommended. You should write and record in your journal anything that is related to your forex trading. It is good to start it with your goals and reasons on why you want to trade binary options. You should also write your observations of the market, any successful trades, and the mistakes you have committed, as well as the opportunities that you have taken and those that have you missed, among other things.

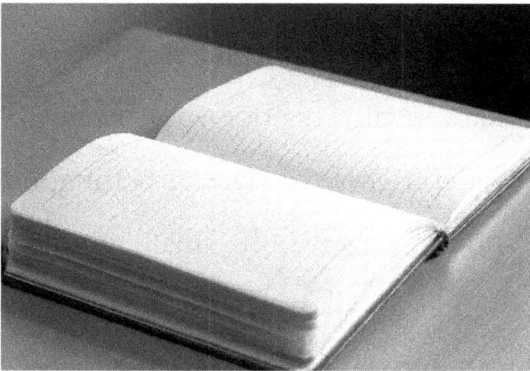

Your journal should show your good and bad experiences. Feel free to express yourself. You do not have to be a professional writer, you simply need to write how you feel and think — and most of all, be honest.

A journal will allow you think outside the box and be a better trader. You will more easily see your mistakes, as well as any adjustments that your strategy needs. If self-control becomes an issue, you can also read your journal, so you will be reminded of why you are trading in the first place. Also, by writing and reading your journal, you can feel more inspired to trade binary options.

Start small

It is tempting to place a high wager, especially if you have researched and analyzed the possible outcome of an underlying asset. However, if you are a beginner, it is highly recommended that you start small. This does not mean that you should simply follow a conservative style of betting, but also means that you should wager only small amounts, preferably the minimum that is allowed on your trading platform. You should test the water first and get a good actual understanding of how binary options work. This is also a good way to gain confidence and an effective way to test your strategy. Even if you get a series of in-the-money, stick to wagering a small amount until you become more experienced and truly ready to increase your wager.

Diversify

Do not invest all your money in a single option. Take advantage of the wide array of assets that you can wager on. This is one of the advantages of trading binary options. You have lots of choices. You can diversify and minimize your risk. After all, no matter how well you have computed or researched the outcome of a particular asset, there is no 100% guarantee that the outcome will be the same as your prediction.

Increase your winning rate

For starters, instead of focusing on how much money you make, focus on increasing your winning rate. Since your broker will not give you a 100% return, you need to have a winning rate of around 60%-70% to earn a profit.

Test your strategy

Never place a wager without testing your strategy many times. It is suicide. Take note also that you do not just test your strategy once or twice, but many times. Even when you make just slight changes in your strategy, you need to test it again. A good way to test your strategy is to use the free virtual credits (demo play) and see how effective your strategy is. Also, when you test your strategy, you need to be open to accept any weaknesses that you can find. Unfortunately, some inexperienced traders keep a blind eye and refuse to accept that something is still wrong with their strategy. Instead, they rush into the game, apply their underdeveloped strategy, and then get disappointed when they lose their money.

Develop your strategy

Coming up with a strategy is one thing, developing a strategy is another. Strategy development is a life-long process. This is because your strategy must be flexible enough and adapt to market changes. When you engage in binary options, you do not deal with a mere random number generator or a robot — no. You have to deal with real people and real businesses on an international scale. Since you are faced with a living market that continues to change and grow, your strategy must also continue to develop and improve.

Have your own understanding of the market

If there is one thing that separates the experts from beginners, that would be having their own understanding of the market. Experts have developed their own view of the market. This view is not necessarily shared by other experts, which means that it may be different from the point of view of another expert. But, this is what makes it fascinating and also proves that the binary options market is truly alive and growing. In the same way, you need to develop your own view or understanding of the market. In the beginning, you will read lots of things about the proper way to analyze a graph, but soon you need to come up with your own way to read a chart and make your own predictions.

Self-control

Just like in everything in life, self-control is important. It is not just about controlling yourself from chasing after your losses or wagering a high amount. It also means that you should control yourself from being too disappointed when you suffer a loss. It means that you have to control yourself and exert serious efforts in research and analysis.

If, at any point, you feel like you are being forced to make a decision, or when you feel that your decision is being unduly influenced by something other than yourself, jus stop and do not commence a trade.

Practice

The only way to truly learn how to trade binary options is by actual practice. No matter how many books you read, it is still actual experience that will make you a better trader. Although binary options seem very simple since you only have two main choices, Call vs. Put, you will soon realize that it is actually much more than that. The thing is, choosing Call over put or vice versa is easy, but knowing which one to choose, where you have to read the graphs, search for patterns, and analyze lots of data and the news is a massive challenge and a big commitment

Practicing does not mean spending hours playing a guessing game. Practicing means analyzing the information that you can gather, placing a bet, and studying what makes the wager a success or a failure. It also means that you should work on improving your system. True practice takes hard work, patience, time, and effort. If you want to have a good career in trading binary options, you need to practice, practice, and practice some more.

Know when to stop

Just as you should know when to make a trade, you should also know when to pack up and call it a day. Although generally anyone above 18 years of age can trade binary options, it is not for everyone. If you notice that binary options only make you lose more money, then stop.

If you are stubborn enough to pursue binary trading despite so many losses, learn to be satisfied with small wagers or even with a demo play. You need to develop a better strategy first. Just as you should know when to stop when you encounter so many losses, you should also know when to stop when you experience a series of successful trades. It is not uncommon to see traders enjoy significant profits only to encounter big and continuous losses. Be sure to withdraw your profits before you hit the ceiling.

Of course, stopping is something that you need to think about seriously because, sometimes, it is even better if you do not stop.

CHAPTER 5: COMMON PITFALLS AND HOW TO AVOID THEM

Many beginners and even intermediate binary traders continue to commit the same mistakes which cause them to lose their money. There are two things you should do to avoid facing such undesirable consequences. First, you should be aware of the pitfalls that many traders often fall into; and second, you should make the necessary adjustment. Although merely avoiding these pitfalls does not guarantee any profit, it can significantly minimize your losses.

Lack of research

If there is one thing that makes binary options different from casino games, it is the presence of factors that greatly influence the outcome. Be sure to do your research before you place a wager.

Applying an untested strategy

Many commit this blunder when they have a tested strategy but during the course of a trade realize that there is an impending loss. However, they also realize a way to improve their strategy. So, what they do is make another trade implementing their new discovery without even testing if their theory will work. Unfortunately, one trade is not always the same as another. Therefore, although making a profit is still possible, the probability of losing remains high. The lesson here is that once you modify your strategy or once you have any new strategy, be sure to test it first using the free virtual credits (demo play). Many times you will feel too lazy to do this, but remember that being lazy is also an effective way to lose your investment.

Trading under pressure

Trading under pressure does not just mean trading right after you have encountered a big loss. It can also occur right after you hit a big payout. Some traders suddenly turn into aggressive betting right after a big win, or even after a serious loss. Again, test your strategy first. Also, do not trade with the money that you need to cover your household bills. Trading when under pressure can blind your rational thinking and turn you into a compulsive gambler.

Using the same strategy

When trading binary options, always remember that you are dealing with a market that is alive. Although you place your wager on particular assets, these assets are run and influenced by real people and real businesses. Just as the market continues to grow, you must also continuously develop your strategy. Coming up with a winning strategy is a life-long process. You must keep on modifying it, and it should be flexible enough to adapt to innumerable market changes.

Another important thing to take note of is this: Do not keep on using the same strategy that has not made you any profit. If you really like such strategy, then make some adjustments. Unfortunately, some traders continue to use the same losing strategy hoping that it will work after some time, and so they just keep on losing. And, even if they win a wager, the profit would not be enough to cover their losses.

Over-investing

Some oft-given gambling advice that is also applicable to trading binary options is: "Only play with the money that you can afford to lose." Do not use the money that you need to payyour electric bill or any other expenses and obligations. Like any business venture, there is no guarantee that getting into binary options will make you any profit. And, although trading binary options has a high-profit potential, it is also a high-risk investment. You can make money quickly, but you can also lose your money just as fast.

Short-term trades

It is common to see a trading period that will only last for 30 seconds or a minute. Although this looks tempting, it is not advisable that you engage in such very short-term trades, unless if you are sure that the trading platform that you use is 100% trustworthy. The reason is that unscrupulous brokers take undue advantage of the short timeline. Usually, when you engage in a short trade, the value of the asset does not fluctuate that much. You may get the right option as much as the official record is concerned, but you would lose the wager. This is because there is a lapse of a few seconds for the platform to record the updated numbers, and these numbers are being continuously updated. This little delay can cost you your whole wager. Fortunately, not all platforms are like this. There are still reputable and reliable binary trading platforms out there.

Over-analyzing

When trading binary options, you do not have to research and analyze the whole market. After all, you cannot possibly study every little detail that takes place in the business world, nor can you measure the market's behavior with certainty.

Although you cannot sacrifice the importance of research and analysis, do not over-analyze things. Take note that no matter how much you read and analyze, there are only two options to choose from.

Accepting the bonus

It is common to see trading platforms that will offer to top up your deposit. They may offer to add as much as 100% of your deposit. So, if you deposit $500, you will have $1,000 in your account. If you think that this is a good deal then you will have to reconsider your decision. After all, no business or trading platform would give out that much money without a catch.

The problem with receiving the bonus is that you will soon have a problem withdrawing your money. Usually, part of the terms and conditions of receiving the bonus is that you need to make a wager equivalent to an amount stipulated in the contract. For example: You will have to wager the free $500 bonus 30 times before you can withdraw your winnings. This means that with $1000 in your account, you will have to wager $15,000 before you can withdraw your winnings. Now, the number of times that the bonus money needs to be wagered can even be as high as 50 times, but it can also be lower than 30. Therefore, be sure to read the terms and conditions as stipulated in the contract regarding the acceptance of the bonus money. Make sure that every stipulation is clear to you. If you find any part of the agreement to be vague, do not hesitate to contact the customer support.

Accepting the bonus money is not always a bad idea. It can be a good decision if it is your first time to engage in trading binary options and you just want to test the waters. Also, if you can come up with a winning strategy that can withstand the consequences of accepting the bonus money, then it might be a good choice to give your consent to the bonus.

Superstitious wagers

Many investors place wagers based on mere superstitions, like placing a big wager on Call on their birthday, thinking that it is the perfect timing to rake in serious profit.

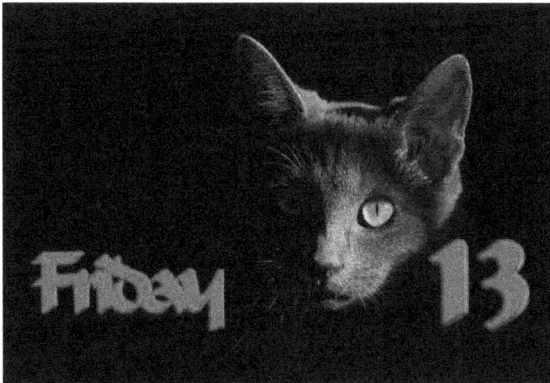

Although there is nothing really wrong about this, you should at least do some study as to which asset you are going to place that wager. Although many gamblers and investors observe superstitious beliefs, do not forget your responsibilities. Such beliefs are not a substitute for hard work.

Relying on "expert" advice

Here is something to take note of: Many of the so-called "experts" have more losses than profits. The sad truth is that many of these "experts" are scams and hacks who just market themselves to be an "expert" but lack the maturity of a true binary options trader. Also, even real experts still commit mistakes, which is normal. Again, improving one's strategy is a life-long process because the market simply does not end.

A good thing that you can do is to know as much "expert" advice as you can. You do this not to be told what to do, but simply to see how your own decision matches up against the pieces of advice from so-called "experts." Although the articles written by the "experts" would be your allies in the beginning because they can help explain to you the basics of binary options, you will soon realize that you can come up with a better output and explanation. When that day arrives, take it as a good sign. It means that you have developed your own understanding of binary options and that there is a potential for you to become a real expert.

Beginner, intermediate, or an advanced trader?

Do not worry whether you should consider yourself a beginner or intermediate trader, and when you can call yourself an advanced binary options trader. The title does not matter. And although passion is important, how much passion that you have for trading binary options would not matter in the end. What matters is how much money you have made, if any. Remember that trading binary options is an investment. It is a business step to earn a profit.

Emotional trader

Do not be an emotional trader. You need to be sure that every wager that you make is backed up with reasons based on sufficient research and analysis. Some binary options traders end up as mere gamblers who place their bets merely based on impulse or mere guesswork. Also, do not be too hard on yourself when you encounter a loss or even a series of losses. And although it is good to have passionate in what you do, never allow your passion to blind your rational and logical thinking.

Increasing the wager without sufficient funds

The moment you increase your wager, you will be using a higher percentage of your total funds. If you lose a single bet, ideally, you should not go back to your previous wager, which was smaller in amount. This is especially true if you increase the amount of your bet significantly; for example, from $10 into $50.

The reason is that you will have to win more times just to get back the single big bet that you lost. The rule here is that once you increase the amount of your wager, your funds must be big enough to withstand it without you having to go back to a smaller wager. Otherwise, if the wager with an increased bet loses, you will only be chasing after that single significant loss using smaller wagers.

Not minimizing your risks

The way to minimize your losses is to minimize your risks. Every time you commence a trade, you risk something. One way of minimizing your risks is by using conservative betting. Of course, you can also switch to an aggressive style of betting, but do not use an aggressive strategy like the Martingale for a long period of time. Another way to minimize your risk is by withdrawing your profit, or at least a part of it. And, of course, an effective way to minimize your losses is by focusing on your success rate and improving your strategy.

Making decisions in a rush

Avoid making decisions in a rush. For example: If, while trading, you realize a good adjustment to your strategy, do not decide to change your strategy right away and apply your new theory. Also, if you suddenly realize that your strategy is working and that you can now increase your wager on the next trade, do not do it immediately. Remember: A single wrong decision can snuff out all your profits and investment in an instant.

Greed

Greed has sent so many gamblers and investors into bankruptcy. If you have a good strategy that can give you small yet regular profits, then do not change it. Some investors do not acknowledge small returns and only focus on strategies that can give them a big amount. The problem here is that the risk increases as the amount of potential profit also increases. Therefore, be satisfied with small profits, provided that it is regular. After all, once you are sure that your strategy can guarantee, or at least have a high probability of generating profit, you can always fund your account with more money and increase the amount of your wager.

Chasing your losses

Never chase after your losses. If you do, there is a higher risk of losing all your money. Most traders and gamblers tend to chase their losses by using aggressive bets right after they experience a bad loss. The problem here is that you continue to use the same losing strategy and your funds may not be big enough to handle the big wagers. Instead of chasing after your losses, focus on the profits that you have already made and try to find ways to earn more. Focus on developing your strategy to gain continuous profit and not on getting back what you have lost.

Going all in

Sometimes, when you experience too many losses in succession, it can be tempting to just give up by betting all the funds left in your account in a single trade. Of course, if such wager is backed up with a heavy research then it may be considered a good choice. However, if the only reason why you bet everything in one trade is because your fighting spirit has given up, it would be better if you do not place any wager at all. Instead, just withdraw the remaining funds. If you just want to gamble, it is better to gamble at a casino so you can get a higher payout if you get a favorable outcome.

CONCLUSION

Thank for making it through to the end of this book, let's hope it was informative and able to provide you with all of the tools you need to achieve your goals whatever they may be.

The next step is to apply everything that you have learned. So, open an account today, start trading binary options, and rake in serious profits!

Binary Options: The Ultimate Guide to Binary Options: Uncovering Binary Options Profit Making Secrets

Description

While binary options are often billed as one of the easiest ways to start investing your hard-earned money, the truth of the matter is that they can be just as tricky and devious as any other investment market investing strategy. If you have already dipped your toes into binary options trading and you are looking for a way to ensure you will not lose your shirt in the process then *Binary Options: The Ultimate Guide to Binary Options: Uncovering Binary Options Profit Making Secrets* is the book that you have been waiting for.

While the fluid nature of many different types of investments means that there is no gray room available when it comes to being successful or not, binary options are an all or nothing proposition that asks the question if a certain underlying asset is going to be above or below a specific price at a given time. This unique duality means that traders do not need to worry about changes over time or to hold onto an investment for longer than it takes for the given price to reach a specific threshold. Unfortunately, there is as little wiggle room when it comes to failure as there is for success which is why it is so important to understand as much about a given underlying asset as possible before taking the plunge.

This is where *Binary Options: The Ultimate Guide to Binary Options: Uncovering Binary Options Profit Making Secrets* comes in as it contains everything you need to know in order to ensure that when the time comes to put your money where your mouth is you can do so with confidence. It does not matter if you prefer a trading style that is high risk and high reward or something that is more risk-adverse and reliable, inside you will find plenty of tips and tricks that are sure to fortify your trading style and turn more of your trades into the right trades at the right time. Don't wait, get ready to get started securing your financial legacy and buy this book today!

Inside you will find

- Trading strategies that are well tested and have been proven successful time and again by experts in the field along with suggestions designed to help you make the most of them once you put them to work.

- Quick and easy tips and tricks that are virtually guaranteed to help you to improve your overall successful trade percentage practically overnight.

- Common mistakes that are made by binary options traders at all levels and the easiest way to ensure that you do not succumb to them without even realizing.

- How to read the trends that are taking place related to a wide variety of underlying assets as well as to make use of this knowledge to find binary options trading success time and again.

- The most important external factors to consider regardless of which type of underlying assets you favor.

- *And more...*

INTRODUCTION

Congratulations on downloading *Binary Options: The Ultimate Guide to Binary Options* and thank you for doing so. While jumping into binary options trading is a relatively straightforward process, finding success there in the long term can be a much more challenging and convoluted as if you are not careful a few poor choices can sink your trading career before it ever really gets off the ground.

As such, to help you make the most of your time spent trading binary options, the following chapters will discuss virtually everything you need to ensure that are successfully able to stick around until you can confidently call yourself an expert trader. First, you will learn about many of the hard and fast rules you should keep in mind when trading in binary options as well as actions that you are going to want to avoid at all costs. From there, you will learn how to analyze underlying assets related to binary options through the two types of analysis, both fundamental and technical, including their various strengths and weaknesses.

After learning how to spot a promising trade, you will learn how to follow through on it thanks to a wide variety of strategies that are going to be useful in many different situations. Finally, you will learn plenty of tips and tricks to help you to take your binary options game to the next level. You will also be learning about common mistakes that traders of all skill levels come across. This book also includes the best ways to avoid these common errors.

There are plenty of books on this subject on the market. Thanks again for choosing us! Every effort was made to ensure it is full of as much useful information as possible, please enjoy!

Chapter 1: Binary Options: Trading Do's and Don'ts

Do's

Know when to go against your trading plan: One of the first things to do when you begin regularly trading binary options is to determine which trading plan works best for you. Your decision will be based on your trading goals, your overall level of risk-aversion and the amount of time you have to devote to trading. It is important to understand that you will run into situations where your plan simply doesn't work. There will be times when you find yourself in a stressful position where none of your previous research seems to help. This stress may stem from a particularly bullish market sentiment. You are going to need to be ready to put the book down to salvage the trade you are getting ready to make or, even worse, have already made.

While you should not be afraid to go against your plan when the situation calls for it, remember it is equally important to ensure that the information you have on the market does not suddenly change. If this occurs, your current plan will be irrelevant for the moment. Make sure emotion is not clouding your judgment of the situation. It is easy to get wrapped up in your emotions and want to go against your plan. Just remember, 9 times out of 10 your plan is going to be the best chance you have of being successful so don't discard it lightly.

Keep emotions out of the equation: While it does not take an expert trader to understand that emotions have no place in a successful trader's repertoire, understanding this fact and using it as a springboard to systematically remove all emotion from your trading experience are two very different things. Emotional removal can be especially difficult if you try to eliminate all emotion at once, which is why it is more productive to go through and cut them out one at a time.

For many traders, the most powerful emotion they come into contact with on a regular basis is anger which is likely responsible for their continuously failed trades. While it is natural to feel angry when you properly execute your plan only to have things go wrong unexpectedly, it is important not to let this anger cause you to suffer additional losses in a misguided attempt to get back at the market for causing your first trade to go poorly. As such, it is imperative to work on seeing the big picture when trading. Understand that losing trades are a part of the process. They are only truly relevant if the losses begin to outperform successful trades to the point where your successful trade percentage drops below 50 percent. As long as your trading percentage remains profitable, then you can think of failed trades as part of the plan.

The second emotion that you want to avoid at all costs is fear. Fear makes it much harder to react to split-second decisions that are often required in order to mitigate loss or ensure that a profitable trade makes as much as possible without exposing you to additional risk. While natural fear is something that will go away on its own as you become a more confident trader, early on you can mitigate its influence by never starting a trade that you cannot afford to lose. The best way to ensure that this is the case is to never make a trade that requires you to put down more than 2 percent of your total available investment capital at a time. This way you would need to make 50 bad trades in a row in order to push yourself out of the game. If this situation does occur, there are likely better ways to invest your money.

Strive to mitigate risk: While you are going to need to come to terms with the fact that any binary options trade is going to contain some level of risk, it is important not to court it unnecessarily either. The best way to ensure that you have mitigated the inherent danger in any trade as much as possible is simply do your homework. Doing so will stop you from jumping into any given trade based on a gut feeling or even worse, from a mere whim. Before you go ahead and make any decision, it is important to look at the potential trade from all of the angles. The different perspectives will ensure that you have a clear idea of how likely it is that the trade will turn out in your favor as well as the opposite, an unfavorable trade.

Don'ts

Don't underestimate the importance of a little extra knowledge: When taken at face value it can be easy to assume that binary options trading is one of the simplest ways to get into the trading world. The information is a faulty premise. However, a few days of trial and error trading is sure to elucidate. Analyze the market and work to utilize what you have successfully learned. Remember there is always going to be new information to absorb like some small altered detail of the financial market which could make a tremendous impact on your plan. The moment that you stop learning all you can about the underlying assets that you are trading is the time that your successful trade percentage is going to start to drop. Keep your finger on the pulse of the markets that you favor, and you will see success if you keep at it, guaranteed.

Don't equate a practice account to the real thing: While many sources recommend starting with a demo account or using one to practice new potential strategies, the truth of the matter is trading with fake money negates an important aspect of the real process. Namely, learning to deal with the added stress that comes with putting your money on the line and taking your chances as a result. Keep the right mindset, even when the going gets rough. Doing so is a vital part of being a successful trader. A plan that works for a demo account might suddenly fall apart if you cannot keep it together when the money is on the line.

As such, it is best to practice with small trades that won't negatively affect your total trading bankroll too drastically if things do not work out according to plan. Practice will allow you to experience at least a version of what it will be like when you start making larger trades so that you are not caught off guard by your emotional response when it matters most.

Don't get too comfortable: Once you develop a successful trading plan, it can be easy to put the process of trading on autopilot and expect things to remain the same as long as you stick to your plan. Unfortunately, things rarely work out this way and the only way to truly find success is to be constantly ready to critique your strategy. Your awareness will ensure that you are going into each day willing to create a new plan for success. This is not to say that you should be radically altering what works. After all, if it's not broken, there is no reason to fix it. You just need to be aware of changes that may occur over time. Ensure that your plan is still going to work as expected before you get ready to make your next trade. Remember, the only true constant in the market is change and only by utilizing this fact to your advantage can you ever truly be successful as a binary options trader.

CHAPTER 2: FUNDAMENTAL ANALYSIS

To make the right choices when it comes to assessing potential underlying assets that are related to a given binary option, it is important to have as much information available to you as possible. There are two primary ways of gathering these details, either fundamental analysis or technical analysis. Of the two, fundamental analysis is used more frequently though technical analysis has experienced somewhat of a resurgence in the past few decades. Both types of analysis are useful when it comes to making the right choices in binary options, though the way they do so is dramatically different. Fundamental analysis is all about looking at the big picture as a whole while technical analysis focuses on the current price of the underlying asset in question and how that price compares to the historical information that is currently available.

While technical analysis is the more complicated of the two, fundamental analysis can often take longer to perform because it concerns itself with a wider variety of data, some of which is not always readily available. The goal of fundamental analysis is to scour available information to find underlying assets that are currently undervalued. The strategy allows investors to make the right choices when it comes to making trades that are more likely to expire in the money and thus generate a healthy payout in the process.

Fundamental analysis is useful regardless of what types of underlying assets you favor because none of them exist in a vacuum. The ultimate goal of fundamental analysis is to find instances of assets that have yet to catch up to current market conditions and then use that disparity to cash in while the market is in a state of flux. While the asset or assets that you are watching may change, the steps for analyzing them are always going to remain the same and are outlined in detail below.

Find a baseline: To determine how new information is going to affect the underlying assets you favor, the first thing you are going to need to do is to identify the overall baseline for the asset in question when the market is in a relative state of balance. Only by understanding the baseline of the property in question will you then be able to accurately determine when changes have occurred (or are likely to occur). The baseline will then make it worth your while to set up binary options trades.

In order to establish a reliable baseline, the first thing that you are going to want to do is to consider any macro or microeconomic policies that may have a natural effect on the underlying assets that you favor, backed up by historical data showing how certain relevant events have impacted the price in the past. When it comes to determining how new events are likely to affect the underlying asset, the best way to do so is to consider previous events as past market behavior is the best indicator of future potential behavior in most instances.

With the historical precedent clearly established, the next step is finding out the current phase of the asset. Every underlying asset can be classified into one of the six distinct phases. Each phase the underlying asset is currently in will determine what tactic you should take when approaching it for trade purposes.

The first and most profitable phase is the boom phase which is known for its large amount of available liquidity along with a historically low level of volatility. On the other hand, if the asset is currently in a bust phase, then it will have a high degree of volatility coupled with a low level of available liquidity. The bust phase is particularly unprofitable when it comes to utilizing binary options as the odds of a trade ending in the money are going to be lower than during any other phase. Each of the two primary phases also then has a pair of lesser phases depending on how long it has been in the phase in question.

Post-boom or post-bust phases show that the boom or bust phases have just about worn out its welcome and that the other major phase is on the way while pre-boom or bust phases indicate that the major phase in question will soon be arriving. There is still money to be made during these lesser phases; it just takes a more sophisticated approach and a greater degree of micromanaging to make it happen. Regardless of the phase, your underlying asset is currently in, understanding the specifics behind it and what caused this to occur in the first place is crucial to making appropriate binary options decisions.

The most reliable way to determine the current phase is to identify the current state of the asset in question by checking with major organizational bodies that deal with it and determine their current level of strength or weakness. If the results are relatively weak, then you can logically infer that the asset is in a bust phase, though if the general market scuttlebutt is that things are improving, then it might be a post-bust phase instead. Likewise, if the state of the underlying asset is above the historical baseline, then you can infer that a boom phase is on its way, if not already here. Remember, the sooner that you get a clear understanding of what phase is coming next, the greater the likelihood of a high payout of the dividends you have set as your goal.

Based on your research, if you are confident that a phase shift is on the horizon, but you do not know when it will get here, then it may be in your best interest to focus on the underlying assets which provide a smaller scattering of leverage points. The underlying assets are more likely to generate a dividend in the short term, while you simultaneously consider the types of trades you can make that will come to fruition in the long term. Alternately, if you are relatively confident that a new phase has just begun, you can safely take on trades with a greater overall level of risk as it is less likely that things will change before they come to fruition.

Be aware of worldwide considerations: With a general idea of the historical baseline for the asset in question as well as its current phase, you will then want to take into account the economic conditions that are happening worldwide and how they may begin to affect the underlying assets that you prefer. While it does not take much effort to determine the general state of these economic conditions, a broad overview is much less likely to give you an edge over your competition when compared to a more precise and well-considered approach that considers details that the more casual observer is likely going to gloss over.

While different assets are going to be affected by various comings and goings taking place in the world as a whole, a good place to start is always going to be in the technology sector as technological advancements are one of the most surefire events that shake up the economic status quo. New technology is going to start upsetting the status quo almost as soon as it gains wide acceptance. The unsettlement happens if it is disruptive of a currently long-standing economic powerhouse and will continue to do so until its existence is so common that it is considered an everyday part of life. At any point in between the chaos, you have a chance to take advantage of the disparity.

Additionally, you are going to want to keep in mind any legal mandates or policy biases that may interact with your preferred underlying asset in either a positive or a negative way. Failing to take into account the potential policy changes from the federal level can leave you blindsided by unexpected changes that can hamstring your plan when it comes time to execute on the information that you have gained.

Put it all together: Once you have a clear idea of what the market should look like as well as what may be on the horizon, the next step is to put it all together to compare what has been and what might to what the current state of the market is. Not only will this give you a realistic idea of what other investors are going to do if certain events occur the way they have in the past, you will also be able to use these details in order to identify underlying assets that are currently on the cusp of generating the type of movement that you need if you want to utilize them via binary option trades.

The best time to get on board with a new underlying asset is when it is nearing the end of the post-bust period or the end of a post-boom period depending on if you are going to place a call or a put. In these scenarios, you are going to have the greatest access to the freedom of the market and thus have access to the highest overall allowable risk that you are going to find in any market. Remember, the amount of risk that you can successfully handle without an increase in the likelihood of failure is going to start decreasing as soon as the boom or bust phase begins in earnest. It is important to get in as quickly as possible if you hope to maximize your profits.

Understand the relative strength of any given trade: When an underlying asset is experiencing a boom phase, the power of its detailed fundamentals is going to be what determines the way that other investors are going to act when it comes to binary options trading. Be sure to keep in mind the action of others while in the boom phase. The earlier the underlying asset is in the boom phase, the stronger the market surrounding it is going to be. Remember, when it comes to fundamental analysis whatever an underlying asset looks like in the present time is not nearly as important as what it is likely to look like in the future. The best way to determine the details of its future is by keeping an eye on the past statistics. Follow this tendency of the previous stats with careful eyes.

CHAPTER 3: TECHNICAL ANALYSIS

Compared to fundamental analysis, the technical analysis only focuses on a few core principals to accurately predict the way that certain underlying assets are going to behave. First, the technical analysis focuses exclusively on the current market price as it believes the current price of a given underlying asset takes into account everything that fundamental analysis strives to consider. This means the only thing that matters is the present price as it naturally encompasses anything and everything that might have caused the price to reach its current point.

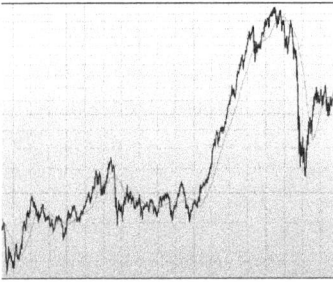

Other than that, the only thing you are going to need to study are the past market trends as they are typically going to be a relatively straightforward way to determine what future trends are going to look like. While using the past to predict the future is never going to be foolproof, when it is coupled with the understanding of the mentality of the market it can be a surprisingly effective way to create accurate predictions as long as you take them with a grain of salt.

Understanding Price Charts

A key part of technical analysis is known as a price chart. This is simply a graph with both an x and y-axis that measures the price of an underlying asset with the price on the vertical axis and time on the horizontal axis. There are several different types of price charts including the bar graph, tick chart, line chart, candlestick chart, point and figure chart, Renko chart, the Kagi chart, and the Heikin-Ashi chart. While all of these charts have their strengths and weaknesses, the most commonly used charts are the bar graph, the point and figure chart, the line chart and the candlestick chart. The graphs are further explained in detail below.

Line chart: The line chart is the easiest type of technical analysis chart to read because it only looks at the price information of a given underlying asset in the form of the price at the close of the day over a predetermined period. The lines in question are generated by the change in the price of the underlying asset over several days with each price getting its own point. When utilizing this type of chart, you are going to want to keep in mind that they are not an accurate representation of the range that the given asset experienced in a given day which means that highs and lows will not be on display. Nevertheless, the closing point is an important consideration when it comes to accurately determining the right choices to make with binary options which make this chart an important one to consider.

Bar chart: The bar chart expands upon the information provided by the line chart by adding in vertical lines that provide a visual representation of several different data points. The bottom and top of each line represent the various highs and lows an underlying asset saw over a set period with the closing point indicated by the dash that shows up on the right side of every bar. What's more, the dash on the left end of the bar shows off the daily starting point as well. When the opening price ends up below the closing price, then the bar will often be shaded black. Then it will be shaded red if the opening price is higher than the closing price.

Candlestick chart: A candlestick chart provides a majority of the same information that a bar shows, it just does so in a more elaborate way. Both charts include a vertical line that illustrates the range of an underlying asset over a prespecified period of time, but a candlestick chart then expands on these details by adding a wide bar which runs along the first vertical line to indicate the range of difference the asset experienced between open and close.

Furthermore, candlestick charts are typically colored to provide additional information though the colors tend to vary from trading platform to trading platform. Whichever colors they choose, a pair of colors will show when a specific day was negative or when it ended with positive movement. If the price of an underlying asset increases to the point that the end of day price beats the start of day price, then the bar is often white or clear. If the ending price is beneath the opening price, then the bar is often red or black. Additionally, if the price of the underlying asset beats the 24-hour high mark, though it still ends below the starting price, then it will be filled in with a third color.

Point and figure chart: The point and figure charts are not as popular as it once was though it has been in continuous use for the past 100 years and can still be useful in certain situations today. This chart can accurately reflect the movement of the price of an underlying asset without as much detail regarding time spent or volume of trades made. Essentially it is a way to see the movement of price without dealing with the noise that comes along with analyzing any market. It is an excellent way to determine if the other charts are utilizing information that is skewing the overall data in an ineffective way.

It is very easy to visually identify a point and figure chart because it contains lines of Os and Xs rather than the now standard points and lines. The Xs show positive trends and the Os show negative trends while the number and letters that line the bottom of the chart show date estimates as well as the months that are being charted. Additionally, this type of chart allows you to set additional criteria based on what exactly it is that you are looking for. For example, you can add criteria to indicate the amount of movement that will be required for an O to turn into an X or vice versa. Finally, trends are marked by a shift to the right as they change over time.

Understanding Range and Trends

When it comes to utilizing technical analysis properly, one of the key things that you will need to consider is if you are going to trade based on trends primarily or if you are going to trade based on range. While both range and trend are aspects of the price of an underlying asset, they are virtually opposites of one another, so you will need to commit to one if you hope to utilize technical analysis properly. Either specific can lead to success when trading binary options, though trend is the more popular out of the two nowadays.

Trend: Trading based on trend means that you are going to be keeping an eye out for what a majority of the investors in the market (or markets) you favor are currently doing, and then follow in their footsteps. Trend can move in both positive and negative directions with indicators of positive trends including things like lows that are higher than the traditional average while negative trends are typically personified by highs that are lower than the traditional average. Regardless of whether a trend is positive or negative, the earlier that you lock on to what the prevailing trend is the greater your chance at generating profits is going to be.

Once you understand what the current trend is likely to be, you are going to want to set up your binary options to take advantage of this fact as quickly as possible and then keep at it, ideally until the moment just before the trend begins to swing back in the opposite direction. While this is a simple idea in theory, in practice it can be quite difficult to time the shift for maximum profits which is why trading based on trend is considered a type of trading that is heavy invested in micromanagement.

Overall, trading on trend is likely to generate a greater number of unsuccessful trades than some of the others. Though, the gains that you do see will typically be larger than those of other strategies which should, in theory, balance things out and leave you sitting with a net gain overall. If you are too risk-adverse for this to seem like a great system, then you may find more success trading based on range instead. When trading based on trend, it is important to always keep to a strict limit when it comes to individual trades to ensure that you do not accidentally end up losing more than you can afford. Don't forget; it is always better to miss out on a potential gain by sticking to manageable trade amounts rather than risking your bankroll and losing everything in one fell swoop.

Range: Trading based on the range is the opposite of trading based on the trend in several important ways. The first of these is that it offers up a much smaller overall level of risk, though the potential for gain is likewise mitigated as well.

Range makes no special distinction when it comes to the direction an underlying asset moves because the logic behind range trading states that the price of the property is always likely to return to at or near the point it originally started at. As such, it is common for range traders to bet on the fact that prices will move the same levels numerous times which means the skilled trader can trade these same levels time and again.

Another key fact about trading based on range is that it is not as important to find the best entry point possible as it is to find a situation where you can build towards a strong trading position. Unlike trading based on trend, it is better to stick with larger overall trades assuming you have the bankroll to hold out until profits begin to generate.

The Importance of Resistance and Support

The concepts of both resistance and support are imperative when it comes to utilizing technical analysis successfully. While these concepts might seem too complicated to parse easily at first, with practice, you will find that it becomes easier and easier to put the theory into practice. Essentially, resistance can be thought of the point at which the price of a given asset hits the ceiling of its positive growth while support can be thought of as the floor past which it is unlike to continue to drop.

Trend lines: While the given floor and ceiling for the price of a particular underlying asset is going to change on a regular basis, understanding when these changes are likely to occur, as well as why they do so, is what separates good binary options traders from amazing binary options traders. The easiest way to start understanding the intricacies of support and resistance is through the use of what are known as trend lines.

As the market trends upward, additional resistance levels are going to be created as the upward movement of the asset in question begins to slow before ultimately starting to slip back in the other direction. This tends to occur as uncertainty mounts around the fact that the given asset can continue rising in value. The rising level leads to the creation of what is known as a short-term top which equates to a price plateau that temporarily caps the current movement pattern.

The plateau can be seen in the charts as the point where the trendline broadens in preparation for its eventual and inevitable turn back the way it came. Additionally, it is important to keep in mind that the trendline itself can often add support to the price of the underlying asset for a prolonged period, especially if overall trade volume is at a low point.

If the market related to the underlying asset in question is trending downward overall, then it is important to keep an eye out for a pair of peaks that may develop at a downward angle along with a trendline that brings those two peaks together. The closer the price gets to the trend line, the more likely it will be for indicators that point out the previous low-point is about to be overtaken. If the current trendline is close to reaching either the floor or ceiling, it is important to keep in mind that it is considered unlikely that the price will continue past the point in question unless the trend it is following is adamant. This means that the level of support and resistance naturally create an ideal entry and exit points when it comes to most underlying assets.

Round price levels: Finally, when it comes to determining the current levels of support or resistance then you can be safe in assuming that the points where the price stagnates are typically going to be round numbers. What this means in a practical sense is that there will likely be several repeat positions at or around the figures in question for both the level of resistance as well as the degree of support. You can now be fairly confident that the price will not creep past these numbers.

CHAPTER 4: STRATEGIES FOR SUCCESS

Pinocchio strategy: The Pinocchio strategy is an ideal strategy to use during technical analysis when you come across a candle bar that contains both a small body and an abnormally long wick. Also known as a pin bar, this type of bar is much like the puppet it is named after in that the longer the wick grows, the more likely it is that the bar is providing you with inaccurate information.

When you are dealing with an extremely long wick, then you can safely assume that the price of the underlying asset has moved about as far as it is ever going to make progress in a specific direction and that it is sure to turn back the other direction sooner rather than later. When you come across this type of bar, then you know that it is time to start trading against the majority as things are likely to change, and soon. Once the wick starts to decrease in size, you are then going to want to set a prediction on a call, and when it starts to increase again, you will want to change that prediction to a put.

Reversal strategy: This strategy works based on the idea that if an asset is currently moving in a specific direction, then it is only a matter of time before it turns back around and moves in the other direction because the market ultimately aims for balance and self-regulates from extreme highs or extreme lows. Thus, when you see an asset moving to one extreme or another, you can get a jump on the competition by predicting what is certain to happen eventually.

For this strategy to work, you are going to want to predict either a call or a put based on the current situation and any additional information you may have been able to gather from relevant sources. You will find this strategy to be extremely effective during periods of rapid asset movement because the speed with which it moved in one direction is quite often the speed with which it will move back in the other direction as well. You will find that once you understand the patterns that a given asset goes through you will then be able to more easily determine when the peak of a given asset has been reached. Ultimately, you can continue to use this strategy while reaping the benefits of the effectiveness without exposing you to any extra risk.

Martingale betting strategy: This strategy is an excellent choice for instances when you are relatively unconfident in the current state of the market, and you are interested in watching a given investment grow so that you can take advantage of that fact. This type of strategy is also relatively unique in that it will allow you to increase a given investment each time that you choose incorrectly until you ultimately come out on the winning side. For example, if you start by putting down $30 and then lose your investment, the next time you would put down $40 and so on and so forth until you come out ahead. Each loss will then allow you to learn more about the market until you can make a larger investment with greater confidence in the side you chose.

This strategy is sure to appeal to those who feel comfortable with high-risk investments that have the possibility to generate substantial returns, while those who are risk-adverse are likely going to want to shy away from it for something with a greater chance of a positive return. With that being said, if you are very familiar with the asset you are utilizing this strategy to invest in then you can mitigate a significant amount of the potential risk. More so than many other strategies, the odds of martingale betting depend on you.

Trade the news: Trading various assets based on the news is a common style of binary options trading that sounds simple in theory while typically being much more complicated in practice. On the surface, it involves buying when good news related to a specific asset is released and selling when bad news is revealed, but it is far from an exact science. Unlike more traditional forms of analysis, trading the news leaves more to chance as the only way of getting a clear idea of how much a given piece of news is going to affect an asset price is through practice and plenty of it. This does not mean that there is nothing you can do to increase your odds of success, however, and the following can help you increase your odds of success significantly.

So let's say you know that a specific piece of news is going to be released, but you are not sure if the result is going to be positive or negative to your particular asset. One of the best ways to ensure that you end up on the right side of the resulting asset movement is by setting boundary options. When utilizing a boundary option, you define a pair of target prices, one on either side of the price the asset is currently going for. The boundary creates what is known as a price channel, and as long as the asset moves all the way to one price point or the other, you will successfully take advantage of the situation. However, if the price of the underlying asset remains in the price channel, then you will not profit from what is happening which is why this strategy is best deployed only when you expect a high degree of movement.

Trading the breakout, otherwise known as the period immediately following the release of important news is another popular way to take advantage of a particularly important piece of news. While this strategy is popular in various types of investments, it offers unique challenges when used with binary options as the window for it to be effective can be exceedingly small, anywhere from a few minutes all the way down to as little as 30 seconds.

The biggest swings in asset price are likely to occur during this period which means that you need to be prepared to move quickly to take advantage of other traders who are looking to modify their positions in hopes of minimizing their risk. If you have been doing your homework and have a relatively realistic idea of what the news is going to be, then you can set up a simple high/low option to take advantage of the resulting movement. When setting up this option, you are going to want to choose an extremely short expiration point, also known as the 60-second option.

Finally, if you are already familiar with technical analysis, then you may be able to take advantage of opportunities to trade the news with the help of candlestick formations. If you come across a candlestick with a gap in it, then you can assume that the price of a given asset has quickly moved from one point to another that is much lower or higher than where it started which creates the gap. As price movements are typical of a much more gradual variety, identifying a gap gives you a good idea that something interesting is going on with the particular asset in question.

With practice, identifying a gap can allow you to make several different predictions based on what is going on in the market at the time. First, if you have found a gap during a period where the overall amount of trading volume is quite low, then this is a strong indicator that the market will move to correct the disparity very quickly. This type of gap most frequently occurs when a large trade is made near the end of the day after a majority of traders have already thrown in the towel. As such, the change is not necessarily reflective of the asset's strengths so you can easily set up your trades to take advantage of the fact that things will soon be moving back to normal under normal conditions.

On the other hand, if you find a gap during a part of the day when trade volume is very high, and the previous amount of movement to the asset price has been negligible the this is a strong indicator that a new breakout is occurring which means you have an opportunity for greater than average profits. If you move quickly, you can then take advantage of this fact by trading in the direction that the breakout is moving by predicting the price trend.

Finally, if the gap appears during a period of normal trading volume and the price of the underlying asset is already trending noticeably in a specific direction then the gap is most likely an indicator that the trend is accelerating in the given direction. As such, you can be fairly confident in a prediction that says the trend is going to continue, at least in the short term. Depending on the strength of the trend and the length of time that it has already been in existence you may even be able to confidently make a prediction outside of the short term though you should only do so when the indicators you are following are adamant.

Bull and bear strategy: This is a highly popular strategy that focuses on keeping tabs on rising and declining trend lines in order to find the best times to make a trade. When the line flattens out, you can realistically expect to make a profit by entering a prediction that the price is going to start moving again. For the previously mentioned situation, it is recommended that you use a no-touch option. A no-touch option means you will select a price that the underlying asset is very unlikely to reach. If the trend seems to indicate that the price is going to continue to rise, then you will want to choose a call while if things are declining, then you are going to want to pick a put.

60-second strategy: While trading in 1-minute options might not be as accurate as working in the more standard 15-minute range, it can still be a profitable choice when done properly. The 1-minute range is all about quantity of profits overall quality and if you have a relative tolerance when it comes to the risk and rewards you can generate a significant level of profit in a short period of time.

To utilize this strategy, the first thing that you are going to want to do is to determine the current levels of resistance and support in a market where you have already determined that a reasonable amount of change can be expected to occur within the next minute. This can be done through the use of

Fibonacci retracements or pivot points, both of which your trading platform should be able to calculate automatically.

Once you have found the right market, the next thing you are going to want to do is to set up trades on the first touch level. When it comes to trading in markets that have a higher than average level of essentially meaningless information coming in then you are going to want to focus on generating a higher overall volume of trades to balance everything out. During this process, you are going to want to determine the initial point where the price level is going to be rejected and if it works out as you expect then you will have a better idea of how sound that price level is and can then utilize it in future touches. The result is that you will end up with more accurate setups for future trades that mitigate the noise inherent in short term options.

This is not to say that trading at touches of all types of resistance and support is the right idea either. Instead, it is important to always keep the current price action in mind. This means you will want to factor in momentum, trend direction and the like as well as the personal nature of your exposure to the market in question if you hope to be successful when it comes to utilizing this strategy effectively.

While trading at an overall higher volume is recommended, it is crucial to stay away from setups which do not exist. Keep your emotions intact and remember, it is always better to wait for a trade to come along that you at least have a general idea is going to be successful rather than just trading for the sake of trading. Doing anything else is a little better than gambling, and there are more productive ways of betting if that is what you are interested in doing.

CHAPTER 5: TIPS AND TRICKS

Know your signals and stick to them: When it comes to successfully trading binary options, it is important to be aware of the signals that your underlying asset is going to move in a particular direction. Do not vary from them, except in the grimmest of situations when it is clear that something unexpected has happened that you can only deal with at the moment. As prices are always going to be changing, this means that you are going to want to pick signals that are sensitive enough to provide you with the information that you need while at the same time not being overly susceptible to the point that they are generating false positives.

The best signals can be created in two primary ways either through fundamental analysis or technical analysis. Broadly speaking, the best fundamental analysis signals are created by keeping track of the news, specifically any significant economic news releases which means that tracking common economic comings and goings should be a no brainer. What's more, your trading platform likely already has one built into its user interface. Once you become aware of important economic news such as major earnings reports, you are then going to want to take the time to determine what the report is likely going to say as this will give you an edge over the competition who are likely going to be rushing around to make use of the information after it has been officially released. While this method will often lead to valid signals, it is important to keep in mind that a level of unpredictability should also be expected which means the market could very well move in the opposite direction.

Keep a trading journal: While it might seem to be a waste of time at first, the fact of the matter is maintaining a journal of all of the trades you make can be an extremely effective way to analyze what you are doing right, as well as what you are doing wrong in the game of options trading. While one type of analysis or the other might peak your interest when it comes to trading at the moment, keeping a trading journal will allow you to look at your trading results from a more analytical perspective once you have gotten a little more distance and perspective on what it is that you are doing.

To get the most out of this process, you are going to want to keep track of each trade you make. The best information to collect is the date, the state of the market and the underlying asset that you were basing all of your trades on, whether the trade ended up being profitable or not. Also, keep notes on your emotional and mental state while you were trading. This journal will provide you with the blueprints you need to find patterns in your successes as well as failures in the trading industry. Be careful though, checking this journal daily or weekly will not provide strong enough evidence to acquire a tendency. Stick to once or twice a month to reflect back on the data. The journal entries provide the most help to your success since you will be able to tweak any flaws or weaknesses.

Make a point of never personally investing in the underlying assets you are working with: While it is natural to favor a particular underlying asset or set of properties once you become heavily invested in binary options trading, it is important not to let this investment become an unreasonable bias. If you let yourself get too committed to any one asset, then it can be easy to lose your objectivity which can make it much harder to decide on the on-the-fence decisions which you will be required to make to be a successful trader.

119

This is equally true when it comes to making trades to recoup previous losses as it can be easy to become off tilt once you start trying to make up for mistakes that have already been made instead of looking to future trades with a clean slate. Specifically, you are going to want to avoid making the mistake of doubling down on an asset that has served you well in the past but has since been headed down with no remorse to hypothetically profit from its return to glory should it occur. This is little more than throwing good money after bad, however, and should be avoided whenever possible. The best way to prevent this from happening is to take special pains never to make a trade that you would not have done at the start of the trading day where you were at your best and were thinking clearly.

Keep the mood of the market in mind at all times: Fundamental and technical analysis are all well and good, but they will only take you so far before you run into instances where the market seems to balk at the logical choice and move off in an unexpected direction. This typically happens when the will of the market goes against the status quo thanks to an unexpected outpouring of support from traders who are thinking with their guts instead of their brains. The best way to go about doing this is to keep tabs on what the major players in your market of choice are up to as this will typically act as a litmus test when it comes to the feelings of the market as a whole.

Don't be afraid to wait for the right time to strike: If you find the market in a state where there are several days of robust trading with little downtime in between then, it can be easy to adopt a mindset that you should always be trading if you hope to be successful. In reality, however, this is a damaging mindset as trading too frequently can be more harmful to your bottom line than not trading frequently enough. While it can be easy to feel as though you are missing out by not making trades at all times, the truth is if there isn't much going on in your market of choice, then there is no reason to force it by making trades that aren't going to amount to anything.

Overtrading will often do nothing but cost you transaction fees and even worse, potentially put you in a situation where you miss out on actually useful trades because you were too busy focusing on trades that weren't going anywhere useful. Remember, you can be a successful trader with as few as 3 to 5 quality trades each day, as long as they are the right trades and you carefully consider the pros and cons of them before you commit to anything.

Learn from your mistakes: While it is natural to want to ensure your successful trading percentage is as robust as possible, it is important to keep in mind even the most successful traders on the planet cannot boast a 100 percent successful trade percentage. As such, instead of seeing the trades you make in black or white when it comes to success, it is much more productive to look at failed trades as an excuse to learn from your mistakes instead of discarding them completely.

When a trade does not work out as you expected, take the time to consider why this might have occurred or what signal you might have missed doing better next time. Take the extra time to focus on executing each trade to the fullest extent of your abilities. The next time a trade fails to materialize in the way you expected, you will be confident every stitch of effort was put into making your decision. This will ultimately increase your chance of maximizing profits. After all, sometimes the market moves in mysterious ways, and there is just no way to account for some of these unknown tendencies.

CHAPTER 6: MISTAKES TO AVOID

Avoid discounting volatility: Being aware of the amount of volatility that is currently plaguing a specific market is crucial when to comes to making real investments that are going to end up paying out in your favor in both the short and the long term. Understanding the current level of volatility in the market of your choice is quite simple as all you need to do is consider the stock market as the volatility of all the other markets is likely to reflect the same level of volatility as it does at least 9 times out of 10. The greater the degree of stability that the stock market is experiencing the more confident the majority of traders are going to be across the board which means the overall level of stability is going to more or less remain the same.

A stable stock market is different from a genuinely stable market, however, as there is always going to be an underlying layer of instability no matter what the outward appearance may be. As such, it is always going to be a good idea to plan for the worst while at the same time hoping for the best. A good rule of thumb is that the stronger and more durable a boom phase is, the lower the overall level of volatility is going to remain while the shorter a boom phase is, the more volatile the market is likely to be at the same time.

Avoid choosing the wrong broker: Perhaps more than any other type of trading, selecting the correct binary options broker is crucial to your long-term success. Remember, you are putting your investment capital into their hands which is why it is so important to know what those hands have been up to. It does not take much time or effort to create a website that appears to be on the up and up and the difference between a legitimate broker and one that is only out to scam potential clients are going to be minor in most cases.

Luckily, the internet has a long memory which means that a little cyber-sleuthing should be all that is required to get to the bottom of any potential issues. The first thing that you are going to want to consider is the customer service history of any prospective brokers. When doing so, you are going to want to be sure that they can provide adequate customer service and also that their underlying technology is as fast as possible for when you are trying to make a trade where every second could bring you closer to success or failure. As such, you are going to want to remain on the lookout for complaints stemming from poor customer service.

You are also going to want to take this process one step further and try contacting any potential brokers in person before making any true commitments. You never know when their online service might be down and being able to talk to a live person could be the difference between a major windfall and a significant loss. If you cannot make contact with them with 24 hours of your initial attempt, then you are going to want to look elsewhere. After all, if they are so slow to respond to a potentially new customer then how can you expect them to be responsive once they already have your money. Finally, it is important to choose a broker from a country which can provide oversight and regulation to ensure that you have some form of recourse if, despite your best effort, things still go wrong.

Avoid putting all of your eggs in one basket: While new binary options traders often stick with a single underlying asset while they are learning the ropes, once you make it past this phase it is best to start looking into multiple different assets to ensure that if one segment of the market unexpectedly turns sour, you don't lose all of the trading capital in one fell swoop. Remember, there is plenty of uncertainty in even the calmest of markets as uncertainty is what leads to profit as far as investment is concerned.

When it comes to being successful with binary options a good rule of thumb is that the more diversification your portfolio can handle the better. You may even want to go so far as to utilize different financial advisors or brokers depending on a specialty that each provides. While this will likely be more time consuming than simply sticking with what you know, it will be worth it the first time that things go wrong with one asset and you have saved yourself from a potential financial disaster.

Don't forget it is still about supply and demand: While there is certainly plenty of high-level considerations that can take place when determining what underlying assets to follow and what types of trades to make that doesn't mean that you should forgo the basics of what makes all the various markets tick when you want to be successful in binary options trading. Specifically, it is important always to remember that simple supply and demand is at the root of everything. As such, if you keep an eye out for situations where supply and demand are unbalanced then you can find an easy place to start which you can utilize the more complex strategies discussed in the proceeding chapters to ensure your successful trade percentage remains as high as possible.

Keeping this simple fact in mind means you will be able to spend less time considering possible entry points and devote more time determining the best decisions to make when it comes to making successful trades. Remember, when the supply of a given underlying asset is low, then the prices that it affects are going to be higher which means that a majority of investors are going to be looking to sell while if there is a dearth of available buyers, then the market is going to naturally lean towards buyers. Keep the fundamentals in mind, and you will do better overall, guaranteed.

Don't be afraid to utilize daily limits: It is important to understand the amount of risk you can safely undertake. Understanding this amount is key to being a successful binary options trader in the long term. If you find yourself losing control of your emotions after a day of trades not going according to plan, then you may find it helpful to set daily limits to ensure that you do not end up on tilt. Setting limits to how much of your total investment capital you can lose in a day is an excellent way to prevent a few bad trades from spiraling out of control. This will prevent you to make the types of trades that you would not normally make when you had a clear head and can actually improve your overall successful trade average.

Prevent yourself from getting in your way and causing a small string of bad luck to multiply exponentially. To do this, a good rule of thumb is to limit yourself to losing a full 10 percent of the total trading capital in a single go. Especially if you have a smaller total to start with than you would like. This will give you time to recover from the bad run, and also give the market some time to change and, hopefully, re-center itself so that you research and trading plan can get back on track. Remember, as long as you have a trading plan that is successful more than 50 percent of the time; then you will ultimately succeed in the long run as long as you do not let the occasional losing streak cause you to make mistakes that you otherwise wouldn't.

Don't let unrealistic expectations hold you back: While trading in binary options can net you a tidy return on your investment, it is a game of inches, not of miles. As such, if you are holding out for massive windfalls then not only will you frequently be disappointed no matter how successful your trading plan objectively is, you will likely find yourself taking risks that don't equate to the potential for a reward that they otherwise might. As such it is important to have clear trading objectives before you start trading in a day to keep yourself on the straight and narrow.

When it comes to defining your investment goals, there are several different methods to consider. While aiming to generate the highest level of returns possible or even simply beating the market can be effective, setting goals for your investing can be even more productive in the long term. This strategy emphasizes setting objectives that will help you to reach real-world goals and can make the general funds that you are working with as a binary options trader seem much more concrete. This, in turn, will help you to realistically assess the level of risk that is right for you in a way that has a practical application to your daily life. Instead of shooting for arbitrary benchmarks, this strategy emphasizes things like setting up a retirement nest egg, buying a house or preparing to put a child through college.

In addition to making things seem more real, this type of strategy is more likely to help you save and achieve the goals you are setting by helping you to be more motivated to take modest profits as opposed to striving for higher risk/reward trades that are less likely to be effective in the long term. You will also be able to make different decisions based on the time frame that you are working with to reach your goals in order to ensure that you are always moving forward. Remember, it does not matter if you prefer concrete or abstract goals, the most important thing to remember is that you should always have some goal in mind otherwise your financial health is sure to suffer. If you are unsure of what your trading goals should be then the best course of action is to discuss them with a financial advisor. Even if you do not employ them full time, a single meeting with a trained professional is an excellent way to ensure you are pointed in the right direction.

CONCLUSION

Thank for making it through to the end of *Binary Options: The Ultimate Guide to Binary Options: Uncovering Binary Options Profit Making Secrets*, let's hope it was informative and able to provide you with all of the tools you need to achieve your financial goals whatever it is that they may be. Just because you have finished this book does not mean there is nothing left to learn on the topic, expanding your horizons is the only way to find the mastery you seek.

The next step is to stop reading already and to prepare yourself to do everything that you need to do in order to ensure that your time spent trading binary options is as profitable as possible. With the tips and strategies provided in the previous chapters at your fingertips, you should soon find it easier than ever before to maximize your hard work and dedication and to face down even the unruliest trade in the most logical and efficient way possible.

While you are now better equipped to handle the intricacies of binary options trading than ever before, it is important to keep a realistic viewpoint when it comes to the profits you can expect to see while trading if you hope to be successful in the long run. Major windfalls are going to be few and far between and chasing them is a surefire way to lose any profits you may have made. Rather, it is a much more proficient choice to create a plan that is successful enough to ensure you will win out in the end and stick to it no matter how tempted you might be to deviate from it in one way or another.

No matter what you might feel at the moment, doing your homework and perfectly executing your plan are always going to be the road to greater overall profits. Remember, binary options trading is a marathon, not a sprint, slow and steady wins the race.

BINARY OPTIONS: STRATEGIES ON HOW TO EXCEL TRADING BINARY OPTIONS

DESCRIPTION

Binary options occupy a unique space in the equities markets in that they require less from the trader when it comes to making the trade, yet are no less complicated when it comes to whether or not that trade makes money. In fact, as they are simply a yes/no proposition, binary options trading can actually make it easier to lose money if you aren't careful about the choices you make. If you are familiar with the basics of binary options and are looking for a way to take your trading game to the next level then *Binary Options: Strategies on How to Excel Trading Binary Options* is the book that you have been waiting for.

Inside you will find everything you need to start utilizing the same strategies as the professionals use in order to ensure that every trade you make has the potential to be as profitable as possible. It doesn't matter if you favor momentum strategies or those that favor divergence; Bollinger band indicators or those based on Moving Average Convergence and Divergence, or even if you favor stocks or forex, this book provides the tools you need to find success in binary options trade.

Millions of people around the world are making a profit through trading binary options by simply choosing put or call and there is no reason that you can't be one of them. If you have ever dreamed of being a professional trader then it is time to take that goal out of the realm of idle fancy and put it to work in the real world today. Stop dreaming about financial stability and start working towards it, buy this book today!

Inside you will find

- The pros and cons of using a pure momentum strategy.

- The easiest way to put the quantitative qualitative divergence trading strategy to work for you.

- How to trade via Bollinger bands either in the 1-minute or the 1-hour charts.

- MACD trading strategies for any timeframe or market condition.

- *And more...*

INTRODUCTION

Congratulations on downloading *Binary Options: Strategies on How to Excel Trading Binary Options* and thank you for doing so. Binary options occupy a unique space in the equities markets in that they require less from the trader when it comes to making the trade, yet are no less complicated when it comes to whether or not that trade makes money. In fact, as they are simply a yes/no proposition, binary options trading can actually make it easier to lose money if you aren't careful about the choices you make.

To ensure they are as much of a winning proposition as possible, the following chapters will discuss a wide variety of strategies that can be employed to ensure that the choices you make are the right ones. First you will learn all about momentum and the most common strategy used to bend it to your will. Next, you will learn the details behind BOMS strategies and how to master them. From there you will learn about the importance of divergence and a few of the many possible strategies that you can use to be sure that when it occurs you are ready to profit from it.

From there you will learn how to employ Bollinger bands in options trading in multiple different scenarios as well as the best times to do so. You will also learn all about the Moving Average Convergence Divergence indicator as it applies to binary options and multiple strategies for using it successfully across multiple timeframes. Finally, you will learn about Nadex trading signals and who is best situated to take advantage of them as well as the percentage price oscillator and the stochastic oscillator and how they apply to binary options trades.

There are plenty of books on this subject on the market, thanks again for choosing this one! Every effort was made to ensure it is full of as much useful information as possible, please enjoy!

CHAPTER 1: MOMENTUM STRATEGY

The binary options momentum strategy is based around providing measurements of the relative strength of specific price movements. Essentially, a buy signal to start a new call option is generated when an asset begins to pick up positive movement while a put option is activated when decreasing movement is noted.

This is an effective strategy because momentum changes are often the prelude to significant reversals in price that signify the creation of new trends. As such, learning to identify these events makes it easier to see increased binary option profit but only when you execute in timeframes that are relevant to the significance of the trend that is determined.

The most important feature of this indicator is a point of reference which is located at the 100 level and is used to determine the difference between momentum that is falling and momentum that is rising. Additionally, momentum should be displayed as a single line which means that when upward momentum is registered above the 100 point, then a buy signal is generated. At this point you will want to open a call option based on the underlying asset you are measuring.

On the other hand, if the signal line declines below 100 then you will want to interpret this as an indication to sell. This means you will want to activate a put option based on the same underlying asset. Candlestick formations are a reliable secondary confirmation for the type of critical events that the momentum indicator provides.

Momentum candle

A momentum candle is a candle that has a wick which is approximately twice the size of the previous candle. While you may sometimes get a red candle that is twice the size of a green candle and vice versa, it is important to wait for an additional candle to form in these circumstances as it is possible for a trend to briefly reverse before then beginning to reliably move in the direction indicated by the first momentum candle that follows the overall trend of the underlying asset in question. Additionally, you may want to wait for a second momentum candle of the same type to form to guarantee the trend is forming in the direction you are looking for.

Also known as a momo candle, the momentum candle is important because it indicates a significant movement in price above and beyond the range of the previous candles. The greater the differential between the momentum candle and the previous candle the greater the indication that the price is going to move in the direction the original momentum line predicted. It is common for the momentum candle to appear well before the moving average equalizes with the current price. Occasionally, the moving average and the momentum candle will line up with one another which can add a third level of confluence to the potential trade.

Zero line: The price will very rarely move in one direction without stopping, it tends to come back to previous test areas which are often located within the current momentum candle. Likewise, the price will often come back to the initial breakout point where the momentum candle started, or to other points within the candle. This price movement is often tracked via what are known as zero lines or sometimes zlines.

These lines indicate where many traders who are trading the break of the range then move their stops to and represent a breakeven point. If the price returns to this point these traders won't lose money, but they won't make a profit either. The price will then often continue to move in the direction of the breakout, forming another momentum candle in the process.

In order to take advantage of zero lines you will want to wait until the price has moved to a point where it has taken out a majority of the novice traders who are sniffing around and then trade in the proper direction to generate a profit. While not every momentum candle and zero line will hold long enough to make a profit, if you confirm it using the momentum line then you will find that the price often wicks the zero line before then closing above it assuming the zero line holds. If the next wick then forms in the opposite direction before the close moves in the direction of the momentum then you have a good idea that the price is likely to continue in the direction of the momentum even more.

Mighty Zone: The price frequently turns at around 50 percent of what the momentum candle shows. As a general rule, the area that is between 0 and 50 percent of the momentum candle is known as the mighty zone. This is because, if you utilize the Fibonacci sequence to chart the levels you will see that they experience a high degree of trade volume. The fact that the price often doesn't close beyond this zone can add further confirmation to your momentum trade.

Timeframe: The momentum candle can appear on virtually any timeframe from the 1-minute chart all the way up to the monthly chart. When looking at various timeframes the greater the timeframe chart you notice the momentum candle is, the stronger that momentum is overall as a whole.

Momentum strategy disadvantages

Multiple confirmation points required: Some traders do not appreciate the momentum strategy because it requires two separate candlesticks to verify. This is only really a downside if you are trading in the extreme short term as by the time you get the confirmation you are looking for it could easily be too late. With longer timeframes, this disadvantage is mitigated as you have the time to get the confirmation that you need.

Oscillator: The momentum signal line is an oscillator which can also be considered a drawback. As such, the readings it produces will have a tendency to lag behind the most current market conditions, as such, by the time the oscillator has clearly defined a trend, it is possible that the price will have already entered a different phase. This is a situation that could lose you money if the price has already started moving in the opposite direction that the signal line indicated. This can lead to a binary option entering an out of the money point almost as soon as it is placed. Again, this can be easily mitigated by simply sticking to longer timeframe charts when you will naturally have more information available at your disposal.

Advanced method: The momentum method can easily generate false signals for those who are not exactly sure what it is they are looking for, even if you have a secondary confirmation indicator. As such, they are best used by seasoned traders who have a clear idea of what they are looking for when it comes to a momentum indicator that is strong enough to trade on. Primarily, the biggest thing to consider when you see a put or call indicator is patience as you will never want to execute until the next momentum candle has been generated. Even still, if you can overcome these issues then you will have a powerful tool at your disposal.

CHAPTER 2: BOMS STRATEGIES

The BOMS trading strategy is designed to follow trends when means you will need to utilize other trading skills in order to use it effectively. The tools you will need for this strategy include the exponential moving average, period 34 green, the exponential moving average period 89 red and the Trader's Dynamic Index set to default settings.

Exponential Moving Average (EMA)

EMA is an average that moves and is similar to the standard moving average with the exception that additional importance is placed on the most recent data available. This type of moving average is preferred by many traders as it reacts more quickly to recent price changes than the standard simple moving average.

26-day and 12-day EMAs are the most popular of the shorter variations and they are useful in the creation of many of the most popular indicators, some of which are described in the following chapters. Generally, the longer EMAs are used as primary signal indicators of longer trends. When applied to charts, trading platforms color in different EMAs for ease of use, primarily in green and red.

Technical analysis traders tend to find moving averages extremely useful when they are applied correctly, but they can lead to serious losses if they are misinterpreted. These averages are always lagging indicators which means concessions need to be made when using them in order to not mistake their data for in the moment information. An EMA serves to alleviate much of this issue because of its emphasis on the most recent data. This causes it to stick closely to the price action which means it reacts more quickly than a standard moving average. This is ideal when an EMA is used to help determine an entry point as it allows you to get in on a positive trend as quickly as possible.

EMAs are most frequently used in conjunction with other types of indicators as a way to confirm significant market movement as well as to gauge their validity. It is especially useful for intraday traders and those who trade in markets that tend to move faster. It is also useful when it comes to determining trading bias.

Reading EMA signals: The EMA line indicator will match the direction the market is currently moving in. It is important to watch not only the direction the line moves as well as how quickly it moves. As an example, if the price action of a strong uptrend starts to reverse and flatten then the rate of change between two bars will start to diminish until the indicator line flattens completely and the rate of change reaches 0.

Due to the lagging effect, by this point in time, as well as in the few surrounding bars, the price action is likely to have already reversed. As such, the consistent diminishing rate of change in the EMA can also be used as an indicator which negates the lagging effect even more.

Trader's Dynamic Index

The Trader's Dynamic Index (TDI) is a popular trading indicator that measures volatility in blue in addition to the relative strength index in green , though it also includes a moving average line in red. Additionally, it includes a line for the market baseline in yellow which acts as a trend indicator. All of the other signals work off of the market baseline.

If the green line is above the red line and both of these are also above the yellow line then you will want to trade calls. If the green line is below the red line and they are both below the yellow line then you will want to trade puts. If the market is currently in a weak trend then the blue lines will show support and resistance based on if the underlying asset in question is oversold or overbought. If the green line touches either of these then a reversal or retracement is often immanent.

When it comes to approaching a trade using this system you start by looking at the current location of the yellow line. If the line is moving on an upward trend then you simply look for the point where the green line is above the red line and the crossover point is the entry point you will try and shoot for. If you are looking for puts then the opposite is also true. If the market doesn't currently have much of a clear direction and the yellow line is mostly flat then trades can go successfully in both direction but only if the green line is outside the blue lines before crossing the red and coming back inside the blue lines. Trades will be taken in the direction of the cross.

While complicated to learn, this indicator can easily show you what condition the market is currently in at a glance. It shows volatility, direction and momentum all at once and frees up space in a window that would otherwise need multiple indicators. It is useful to binary options traders as you can determine the correct course of action from just a few pips of movement.

Using the BOMS strategy

BOMS is a trend following strategy so first you are going to want to look at the current trend in the TDI. To define the current trend, you will look at the EMAs, green above red means that an uptrend is in effect so that you want to trade calls and vice versa. Additionally, you are going to want to look for the green line to touch the blue lines. If you are looking at an uptrend then you will want the line to touch the lower volatility band and vice versa. At the point where the green TDI line crosses the red TDI line in an upward direction you will want to enter your call.

When trading a put it is important that the green line touches either the upper or lower volatility band prior to entering the trade. These volatility bands are similar to Bollinger Bands which means when the price touches the upper band it is close to becoming overbought which means that the odds of a downtrend increase. If it touches the lower level then it is oversold and is likely to increase instead. This strategy looks for these oversold or overbought levels but only so they line up with the trend that is identified via the EMAs.

Pros and Cons

Cons: This strategy cannot just be run blindly without taking into consideration the other things that your chart is currently telling you. It is important to look at the big picture when it comes to the higher timeframe charts to determine if the trend you are following is likely to continue long enough for you to make a profit. It is especially vulnerable to signs of exhaustion. With that being said, looking at the overall highs and lows of the market and determining the direction of the trend isn't an especially complicated addition to the process.

Pros: The signals that this strategy provides tend to occur less frequently than those of many other strategies which means you are less likely to overtrade while using it. Additionally, the signals that it provides are almost always reliable, unlike many other strategies that need multiple levels of confirmation. As long as you follow the direction of the EMAs you can easily ensure that you are on the correct side of the trend, then, by waiting for the price to oversell or become overbought you can easily increase the odds that your trade will be profitable.

CHAPTER 3: DIVERGENCE TRADING STRATEGY

Divergences are an extremely popular trading tool thanks to one great advantage which is that they are visible and make purchasing the right binary options fairly straightforward. In order for any of the strategies outlined below to work, you will need to compare the price for the underlying asset to an indicator. These indicators are typically oscillators as trend indicators do not offer real divergence moves.

The oscillator essentially confirms or denies the movement the price is making. Take note, the price has a tendency to make fake moves a large portion of the time so it is better if you stick to a single oscillator at a time. If the oscillator is rising but the price is falling then the divergence is bullish. If the oscillator is falling and the price is rising then the divergence is bearish.

Divergence explained

When there is disagreement between a given indicator and the current price, this phenomenon is referred to as divergence and it can have serious implications when it comes to managing a trade successfully. The amount of agreement or disagreement is always relative so there will be numerous different patterns that can develop in the relationship between the indicator and the price.

Divergence in an uptrend typically occurs when the price hits a point that is above the current high, but the indicator does not recognize it as such. The same goes with lower lows in a downtrend. When divergence occurs, there is always going to be a greater probability of a price retracement. Divergence makes it easier for a trader to react to and recognize the change caused by price action. It also tells you if there is something in the market that is changing that you need to make a decision about such as taking a profit or tightening up a stop loss. Being aware of divergence tends to increase overall profitability by alterting the trader to the situation in order to protect their profits.

Divergence management: Being aware of divergence is key to successful trade management in many situations. The divergence that occurs between an indicator and the price can lead to a pullback before trend continuation. If you see the pivot point for the price that is below the lower trendline this is what is known as a bear trap which occurs when false signals create shorts which then cause the price to quickly reverse. This signal can often be predetermined when the higher low price agrees with the higher low of your chosen indicator.

Divergence always indicates that something is changing but it does not mean that the trend will automatically reverse. It also signals that the trader will need to consider new strategy options including selling a covered call, holding, changing stop loss points or accepting partial profits. While wanting to pick the bottom or the top is often the natural response, this is typically more about satisfying ego than maintaining profits. In order to ensure your trades are consistently profitable you will want to pick the right strategy for what the price is doing, not what you think it is going to do.

Technical divergence: In technical analysis, many indicators often give off multiple trading signals including cross over a center line, divergence and crossing a significant signal line. Of these, divergence is going to be the most complicated to unpack. Negative divergence occurs when the price of an underlying asset is an uptrend and a major indicator such as MACD, ROC or RSI moves downward instead. Alternately, positive divergence occurs when the price hits a downtrend and these indicators begin to rise. It is also important to keep in mind that indicator divergence can occur over a prolonged period of time which means you will always want to check support levels and trendlines in order to confirm a reversal.

Time frame: The expiration time that you will want to choose will be based on the divergence that is spotted as well as the strategy that you use. When you look for a divergence between the oscillator and the price you will always want to check to determine which one is lying as they cannot both be correct. A good rule of thumb is that, when looking at divergence, a trader needs to always stay with the oscillator as the price that is indicating the false move. This is because the oscillator is plotted to take into account the moves of candles that have closed in the past.

As an example, if you plot an oscillator on the screen, you can set the period of that oscillator when it comes to plotting relevant values. If that period is 14 then that means the oscillator will taking into account the last 14 candles before determining the actual value. On the contrary, the price is only ever going to take into account a single candle. As such it is better to stick to the oscillator information as it is more comprehensive.

Timeframe is key in this scenario as if the divergence is occurring on a larger timeframe then choosing the right expiration point can be difficult as it is less likely that you will find an expiration that is big enough to match. Divergence implies picking a bottom or a top and this is the key point to any good trade. Trying to pick one or the other means you have an idea that the market is turning which makes the average divergence extremely visible.

Short term expirations: Ideally you will want to stick to short-term timeframes with the hour charts being the longest you will want to consider as this will keep the expiration dates in a reasonable range. As an example, if you find a divergence in the five-minute chart then even extending it out to the hourly chart can be difficult. On the contrary, if you find a divergence on the hourly chart then you can essentially trade what expiration date you want as the divergence will likely also be on the monthly chart as well

Quantitative Qualitative Divergence trading strategy

To use this strategy, you are going to want to utilize a Quantitative Qualitative estimation tool which smooths existing RSI indicators that results in a pair of lines, one fast and one slow. Its key indicator level is 50 which is used to signal upward or downward trends. This strategy is effective in the 1-minute, 5-minute, 15-minute, 30-minute, 1-hour and 4-hour timeframes. It works in all trading sessions as long as the right signals appear.

The strategy here is to be on the lookout for the point at which indictors start to diverge from the price action. Typically, the price action will then correct itself in the direction the divergence indicates. The key here is to determine the divergence and this is done through the use of a line tool which can trace both the lows and highs of the price as well as the indicator.

This indicator is unique in that it presents a signal line which can move either into the oversold or overbought territories. This means the strategy here is to determine the divergence and then open the trade if the line is in the extreme areas of movement. The QQE is an oscillator indicator which can point out divergence signals as well as the extreme points of price. Success with this indictor relies on the detection of divergence in addition to knowing the right time to set up trades in order to maximize price advantage.

Call entries: You will want to initiate a call when the indicator line is showing overall higher lows than when the price is forming lower lows. You will want to also make use of a trend line to trace out the lows of price action along with the signal line lows. If the lows of the indicator are low enough to be in oversold territory then you will want the next candle that forms on the chart to touch the line you have traced and pull back to it at least once before entering a call once contact is made again.

In this situation, you are going to want to set the trade to expire at the close of the third candle. You will also want to close the trade early if you reach profit territory. It will cause a reduced payout but it is better than running the risk of an abrupt end to the trend that cancels out all of your gains with losses instead.

Put entries: You will want to utilize a put option if the price forms higher highs while the indicator creates lower lows.

You are going to want to trace the highs on price and the indicator line using trend lines. Trace the trend line across the price action highs and then allow the next candle to open. Once it pulls back to this line you are free to initiate the trade at the point of contact assuming the indicator highs form the divergence in overbought territory.

You will want to set the expiration to the close of the third candle. You will also want to close the trade early if you reach profit territory. It will cause a reduced payout but it is better than running the risk of an abrupt end to the trend that cancels out all of your gains with losses instead.

RSI Divergence Strategy

This strategy is based on the RSI indicator which functions as an oscillator and is able to detect overbought or oversold conditions. This makes it qualified to trade divergences as well. The strategy here is to find an indicator that starts to diverge from the price action. Typically, the price action will correct itself in the direction of divergence. The key is to find the divergence which is done through the use of a line tool that can accurately trace the highs and lows of the indicator and the price.

After the divergence has been identified, the trade will then be made off of the trend line which is used to show the high or the lows depending. This indicator is an oscillator which makes it well suited to point out divergence signals as well as extreme price points. The best signals will be found when the indicator line is within the extreme zones of the price. This indicator allows for reliable reversal price action which should generally be just enough to enable a profit turned from a short term trade.

Call entries: You will want to initiate a call when the chart shows an indicator trend line that is forming higher than average lows when the price action trend line is generating lower lows. You will then want to extend the trend line and allow the candle to create a pullback on the price action trend line. When the pullback occurs, you will want to initiate the trade.

With this type of trade, you are going to want to let it run for just two candles or 30 minutes. You will want to close out at the point the second candle closes. You will want to avoid taking an early closure with this strategy, even if you have already turned a profit. The trade should always be allowed to work its way through to a natural conclusion for the most reliable payout.

Put entries: You will want to initiate a put option when the indicator trend line forms lower highs while the price action trend line forms higher highs. You will then want to extend the trend lines and allow the candle to pullback at the price action line. When the candle touches the trend line that connects the highs you will want to initiate a put.

With this type of trade, you are going to want to let it run for just two candles or 30 minutes. You will want to close out at the point the second candle closes. You will want to avoid taking an early closure with this strategy, even if you have already turned a profit. The trade should always be allowed to work its way through to a natural conclusion for the most reliable payout.

CHAPTER 4: BOLLINGER BAND STRATEGIES

Bollinger Bands can be used to trade binary options successfully because they are an effective signal when it comes to markets being overbought or oversold as binary option strategies tend to work best when assets are in one of these extremes as part of a trend.

The default Bollinger band setting is based on the 20-day moving average and has two standard deviations. The upper band is typically 2 standard deviations above the 20-day moving average and the lower band is set 2 standard deviations below the 20-day moving average. The underlying asset then trades between these two prices with oversold levels reaching the lower band and overbought levels toughing the upper band. The band's width then represents the volatility of the underlying asset.

Basic trading strategy: In general, assuming that the market is in an uptrend, you will want to use the overbought readings of the Bollinger band to purchase calls or sell puts depending on the strength of your convictions that the trend will continue as well as your overall aversion to risk. If the price hits the higher of the two bands then you will want to take some profits form the expectation of a revision of mean or through the digestion of the overbought conditions.

If you are more aggressive trader then you may even want to consider buying puts or selling calls. If the market is currently in a downtrend then the choices you make would be reversed.

Bollinger band strategies tend to be the most effective in markets that are currently trendless. Under these market conditions oversold and overbought readings are always going to be more potent. This is due to the fact that competing forces are currently pulling the market in both directions.

It is also important to keep in mind that price has a strong preference towards fluctuation when it comes to the central band. You will need to be able to detect this fact reliably if you want to successfully make use of any of the strategies outlined below. You will also need to be aware that the top band acts as resistance while the bottom one acts as support.

In order to find the best results when it comes to using the Bollinger bands you will want to display them on charts that are at an hourly range or higher as the additional information will make it easier to parse what is really going on. In order to build the best binary option strategies based on the Bollinger bands you will also want to take into consideration that they operate most efficiently under range-trading conditions.

60-second Bollinger Band strategy

This strategy is extremely effective for impatient binary options traders as it can be used for any underlying asset and in any trade session. In order for this strategy to work properly the time frame will be set to 60 seconds and the bands will be set to their standard levels. The expiration time will be 5-minutes.

Buying calls: In order to successfully purchase a call option using this strategy you are going to need to keep an eye out for oversold conditions. If the price of the trading instrument has broken beneath the lower band, you will then be able to anticipate a touch and return with 2 or 3 bands. After this happens you will have the confirmation you are looking for in order to place an order to buy. The best confirmation indicator here is the candlestick reversal pattern.

Buying puts: If you are interested in using this strategy to buy puts you will want to keep an eye out for overbought conditions. You will want to wait until the trading instrument breaks above the upper band in order to anticipate a touch and return within 2 or 3 bands. After this has occurred you will have the confirmation of a downtrend that you are looking for and you can go ahead and place an order to buy. You will want to use a candlestick reversal formation in order to confirm.

60-minute Bollinger Band trading strategy

This strategy makes use of both Bollinger bands as well as a momentum indicator. The time frame for this strategy is 15 minutes while the expiration time is 60 minutes which is enough for 4 complete candles to come into existence. The Bollinger bands will be set to the default 20-day EMA and the upper and lower bands will both have a standard deviation of 2. You will want to set the momentum indicator to 11 periods.

Calls: If you are going to purchase a call option then the trading instrument is going to need to show a price that is greater than the middle band. The momentum indicator will need to be above 100.

Puts: If you are going to purchase a put option then the trading instrument is going to need to be lower than the middle band. The momentum indicator will need to be below 100.

It is important to keep in mind that both conditions will need to be met at the same time in order to provide you with a proper entry point. If there is a cross in the middle Bollinger band but the momentum indicator is still less than 100 you will want to avoid making calls. The same goes for puts if the momentum indicator is higher than 100.

Bollinger band scalp strategy

This is a forex binary options strategy that revolves around the GBP/JPY pair, also known as The Beast or the Dragon. It earned this nickname thanks to its high daily range of anywhere between 100 and 200 pips and the fact that it moves back and forth quite quickly. This means this strategy is not for those with a low risk tolerance or those who are just getting started with binary options trading. With that being said, using this strategy with this pair makes the process smoother and easier to trade due to the fact that you don't need to set a stop loss which would frequently be knocked out due to the volatility. This strategy attempts to scalp this pair in the 1 minute timeframe.

First you are going to want to set your Bollinger bands so that all 3 bands are set to 50 rather than the usual 20. The first band will have a deviation of 2, the second will have a deviation of 3 and the third will have a deviation of 4. Additionally, you will want to add each band to the chart separately. Once this is done you will want to keep an eye out for a touch and break of the first Bollinger band. Additionally, you are going to want to watch the price until it is about half way between the first band and the third. If you can get the price to touch the center band, that is even better though it is not required. After this condition has been met you will want to trade in the opposite direction of the trend in hopes of catching a reversal.

You will want to enter the market with a put option when the price breaks through the first Bollinger band and at least half way through the second. If you are looking to use a call option you will want the price to drop through the first band and go at least half way through the third band.

This strategy completely disregards trends and includes no filters when it comes to determining the type of trend you are working with. This makes it a pure counter trend strategy. This fact, coupled with the high volatility of the Beast and the Dragon pair makes this strategy turn against you in a hurry if you use it at the wrong time. As such, it is important to only utilize it once you have determined the scope of the current trend through the use of additional strategies.

However, if you can successfully identify a ranging market, or at least one that isn't trending too strongly, then the results from this strategy can be quite effective. If the market is ranging then the market price will bounce between the Bollinger bands which is why you can easily make quick money by trading against the prevalent move. It is important to keep in mind that the 1 minute chart is typically full of a lot of trends as well as noise which is exactly what this strategy seeks to exploit.

As long as the price of the underlying asset doesn't move in just one direction for a prolonged period of time, there is money to be made through the use of this strategy. The expiration time of this strategy should typically remain greater than the timeframe of the chart you are using, but in this case a 60 second option can work as well as a slightly longer one.

The biggest variable that this strategy has when it comes to finding success is the trader who makes use of it. If the trader can accurately determine the current state of the market and if it is ranging or trending then major profits are possible. Otherwise, it is likely going to lead to serious losses. As such, it is important to always practice with this strategy before putting it into practice, just to ensure you have it down before opening yourself up to so great of risk.

CHAPTER 5: MOVING AVERAGE CONVERGENCE DIVERGENCE STRATEGIES

Moving average convergence divergence (MACD) is a type of trend following momentum indicator that expounds upon the relationship between two different averages and prices. The MACD can be determined by taking the 26 day EMA and subtracting the 12 day EMA from it. Given this type of construction, the value of the MACD must equal zero each time the two different moving averages cross over one another. A 9 day EMA of the MACD is known as the signal line which is then plotted on top of the MACD where it functions as the trigger for signals to sell or to buy.

The MACD indicator was developed by Gerald Appel in the 1960s as a way of charting momentum by measuring the space between the EMAs. If the space between the two is increasing then momentum is increasing and if the distance is converging then momentum is slowing down. The MACD is extremely popular thanks to its ability to help traders quickly spot changes in short-term momentum.

MACD can be interpreted in 3 main ways. The first of which is the crossover. When the MACD falls underneath the signal line then this creates a bearish signal that says it is time to sell. Alternately, if the MACD is above the signal line then it shows that the price of the underlying asset is about to experience upward momentum. It is common for traders to wait for a confirmed cross that is above the signal line before making a move based on the position in order to ensure that the price isn't going to go through a fake out phase.

The second way the MACD can be interpreted is via divergence which occurs when the price of the underlying asset diverges from the MACD which also signals the end of the current trend. Finally, the third is the dramatic rise which occurs when the MACD experiences a shorter moving average and pulls away from the long-term moving average. This indicates that the underlying asset is currently overbought and will soon be returning to average levels.

Traders are also known to watch for a move that is below or above the 0 line as this will signal how the short-term average is positioned in relation to the long-term average which, in itself, signals upward momentum. If the MACD is lower than 0 then the opposite is true. As such, the 0 line often acts as the resistance and support level indicator. You can draw trendlines on indicators like the 2-line MACD to create a channel of action that can make it easier to determine the strength of a particular trend.

The biggest disadvantage of this type of indicator is that a trader who uses it can easily get whipsawed out of a position several times before they are able to properly capture a strong change in the momentum. This is caused by the lagging aspect of this indicator which can generate multiple transaction signals during a single prolonged move which may result in several unimpressive losses or gains during the rally.

In order to use it properly, traders need to be aware of this whipsaw effect as it can be found in both range-bound and trending markets as all it takes are relatively tiny movements to cause this indicator to change directions quickly. The high number of false signals it generates can also cause traders to take multiple losses when not used correctly. Once you factor commission on top of this it can become quite expensive.

An additional drawback is its inability to make proper comparisons between disparate underlying assets. The MACD typically represents the dollar value of different moving averages, the reading for various different underlying assets adds little insight outside of directly comparing them to one another. If you are interested in doing so then the percentage price oscillator is typically going to be a better choice.

Basic MACD trading strategy

This strategy is useful for standard Put/Call binary potions as well as Touch/No Touch options. The objective here is to find the point where the trend of an underlying asset is likely to change. In order for this strategy to be utilized properly there are several conditions that must be satisfied first. First, the asset must currently be trending. Second, there must be a small pullback by the asset to the level of temporary resistance or support. Additionally, a 50 period EMA must exist as the short-term moving average indicator. This EMA will function as the signal indicator. What's more a 110 period EMA will function as the long-term indicator. It will also function as the resistance and support level. Finally, a MACD histogram will indicate specific changes in the trend.

In order to ensure you have found the proper signals you will want to look for an indication in the histogram for additional changes in the trend. Meanwhile you will also need to ensure that the price of the underlying asset is rebounding from the EMA in the direction that the trend is moving in.

Call entries: You will want to place a call order if the 50 period EMA is above the 100 period EMA. Additionally, the price of the underlying asset will rebound off of the 50 period EMA. Finally, the MACD will show a trend change.

Put entries: You will want to place a put order if the 50 period EMA is below the 110 period EMA. Additionally, the price of the underlying asset will need to pull back from this same EMA. Finally, the MACD will need to show a change in the trend.

Expiration: When it comes to determining the expiration period for trades made through this strategy, they are going to depend on the timeframe that used in the first place. In general, you will want to let the trade run for 4 candlesticks regardless of the chart you focused on. It is important to avoid trading more than 5 percent of your total investment capital while utilizing this strategy in case things swing back in the other direction earlier than anticipated.

5 minute MACD entry strategy

This strategy works in the 5 minutes chart and utilizes a pair of MACDS along with a pair of moving averages. The moving averages are a 50 bar and a 100 bar. The pair of MACDs are both the common 12-day and 26-day with the 9-day signal bar. The first is a histogram and the second is an oscillator. When combined the two can accurately create signals with movements that last from 20 minutes to many hours.

The pair of moving averages are then used to determine the current trend, as well as the type of trade that you will want to make and also as part of the signal for when you will want to enter the trade. In this case, the trend is determined by the position of the moving averages. If the 50 bar moving average is higher than the 100 bar moving average then you know the trend is bullish and you will want to place a call. If the short-term moving average is lower than the long-term moving average then the trend is bearish and you will want to place a put.

The signal to move forward is created when the MACD is either oversold or overbought and is indicated by a crossover at the same time the prices have moved past the moving averages. If the trend is moving downward then you will want to wait for the prices to correct to a point above the moving averages before entering. This will coincide with a signal created by the oscillator MACD which will show on the overbought side of things and create a bearish crossover. This signal, in turn will be predicted by the histogram MACD. The opposite is true for bullish signals.

If used on the 5-minute chart then you will want to target either a 20 or 30 minute expiration point depending on how strong overall you believe the current trend is going to be. If you are using the 30-minute chart then you would set the expiration at between 2 and 3 hours. If you are using the daily charts then you will want to put the expiration point at between 4 days and 1 week. In general, setting the expiration between 4 and 5 candles out is encouraged.

If you feel it necessary, this strategy could benefit from the analysis of multiple time frames. Feel free to add in additional indicators as needed based on the time frames that you prefer.

MACD divergence strategy

This MACD strategy works primarily on the 15-minute chart and takes advantage of the standard divergence signals that the MACD provides. It primarily focuses on the histogram MACD. As the name implies, this strategy focuses on the divergence found in the MACD with the goal of capturing quick moves that come about as the results of reversals and corrections. This strategy uses a single signal along with a single indicator so it can benefit from additional verification through your favorite secondary indicator such as an EMA or a resistance line.

MACD divergence is a contrarian signal that indicates an impending relief rally or market correction. In the charts, this is indicated via a series of lower peaks that occur while the market overall is moving higher. When this occurs, it is a signal that the momentum is weakening and that the market is ready for a pullback or other type of correction. To prepare this strategy you are going to want to add the MACD indicator to the chart along with a fast EMA of 12 and a slow EMA of 26 along with the MACD moving average of 9 applied to the close.

With this strategy, you are going to want to enter long positions if the price indicates a bearish trend while the MACD indicator shows a bullish trend. Likewise, you are going to want to enter a short position when the price shows a bullish trend and the MACD indicator shows a bearish trend. The exit conditions include a stop loss that is near the support level if the entry was long or the resistance level when it was short. You are also going to want to determine a take-profit level that is next to the resistance level if you went long, and next to the support level if you were short. If things start to reverse then you will want to close out the previous position first.

This strategy is particularly useful as it can provide signals that are useful in multiple timeframes, can be used for both bearish and bullish signals and combines well with other techniques to form a sort of second opinion on the current state of the market. The signal is especially easy to spot in the 15-minute chart and works well with an expiration point of between 1 and 4 hours depending on the strength of the trend. If you are interested in using it to trade in the daily or hourly charts you will want to exit at either the end of day or end of the week. It can even extend as long as one month.

When using this strategy it is important to keep in mind that the entry and exit points without a second indicator are going to be somewhat fuzzy. As such it is best to either practice with this strategy before putting it into play or add in a second indicator that will make the overall signals stronger than they are to start.

CHAPTER 6: NADEX TRADING SIGNALS

Nadex is the North American Derivatives Exchange which makes it much more than just an average regulated or unregulated broker. It offers members a fully-regulated CFTC-licensed trading environment which means that the signals it generates are frequently worth listening to. Nadex is the first regulated binary option service provider in the United States. While it is not a classic broker, it is labeled as such, though it operates more like a traditional exchange.

Nadex is significantly different than the binary option brokers who work out of Europe, which are known as CySEC brokers. These brokers act as the sole market-makers in their regions. This means that they act as the house and trade against retail traders. This, in turn, means that a handful of successful European traders can actually drive a CySEC broker out of business.

The United States forbids sole market makers which is why Nadex and other US exchanges have multiple market makers. As such, there is no conflict of interest. As a trader, there are also other differences as well, specifically when it comes to regulation as Nadex is the only fully-regulated binary options destination in the US.

Signal based trades: Nadex trading signals are especially useful because they stem from algorithms that are more advanced than those that many other services use. This is because of a few peculiarities that stem from the signal-based trading that interacts with the nature of the exchange. This is because of a handful of Nadex features that make its signal trading easier, and therefore more profitable, than the signal trading done through other exchanges.

The first of these features is the high payout results that Nadex provides. Because of its nature, Nadex tends to offer naturally higher payouts that a majority of the CySEC exchanges offer. This means that the potential for profits from its trading signals are naturally more profitable, though some traders then choose to act on weaker signals because of their increased profit margins. Additionally, Nadex offers some option types that are not widely available which are naturally suited to more complex trading signals.

Trading Nadex signals: Complex trading signals make it easy to determine the exact spot where a specific underlying asset will be trade at a point in the future. The Nadex 30 strike price feature makes it easy to trade these signals as all you need to do is find a strike price that is close to the predict asset price which Nadex 30 makes easy. There aren't any other brokers out there who offer similar options to the Nadex 30 strike price which naturally makes Nadex the obvious destination for those who are interested in trading those types of signals.

CHAPTER 7: PERCENTAGE PRICE OSCILLATOR STRATEGY

The percent price oscillator (PPO) is an indicator that measures the difference between a pair of moving averages as a percent of a larger overall moving average. This is an ideal indicator for traders who prefer to trade in trends and momentum. Specifically, the PPO measures the difference between the 0-day EMA and the 26 day EMA. The biggest difference between it and the MACD is that the MACD reports the simple difference between these EMAS and the PPO shows this difference as the percentage of the greater whole.

This makes the PPO the ideal indicator when it comes to comparing different underlying assets with different prices. As an example, regardless of the price of an underlying asset, a PPO result of 15 means that the short-term average is 15 percent above the long-term average across the board.

Creating the PPO indicator is quite simple, assuming it is done properly. First, you will want to ensure that you are using the right timeframe which can be anywhere from 15 to 30 minutes. Second, you will want to confirm that the underlying asset you are looking at will display a low level of overall volatility which means the underlying asset is relatively unlikely to change direction while it is being watched. Common assets that are used with this strategy include silver, gold, Exxon, apple, USD/CAD, USD/CHF and EUR/USD.

When the PPO indicator crosses above the zero line into a positive area, the 12 period EMA has cross higher than the 26 period EMA which indicates an upward trend shift. When the PPO cross lower than 0 then the 12 period EMA has crossed lower than the 26 period EMA and the trend is likely reversing downward. If you add another moving average and apply it directly to the PPO then it can apply additional relevant trade signals.

You are going to want to go long when the PPO crosses above 0 and short when it crosses below 0. Additionally, you are going to want to go long when the PPO crosses higher than the 9 day EMA and go short when it crosses below this number. Additionally, you can use the PPO as a warning signal when it comes to an upcoming reversal of an existing trend. You are going to want to keep an eye out for potential divergence as if the PPO isn't climbing when the price is generating new highs then you can assume that a price correction is coming. If the price is dropping but the PPO is staying strong then you can assume a price rally is on the horizon.

In many instances, the PPO is considered the superior indicator to the MACD as it measures the percentage of movements as opposed to the absolutes. Additionally, when an underlying asset makes a very large price move then the MACD levels tend to increase based solely on that rising price which can then lead to divergence anomalies. As an example, assume that a given stock moves from about $250 to about $460. This would cause the MACD to move in a higher-high direction along with the price without creating any noticeable divergence. On the other hand, the PPO would create new highs which would then adequately warns of the price correction which is likely to follow such a major move.

Basic PPO strategy: In this strategy, the PPO is created via a 12 period EMA that is then subtracted from the 26 period EMA and this number is then divided by the 26 period EMA before the result is multiplied by 100. The signal line in this instance is the 9 period EMA of the PPO. The histogram for this PPO is equal to the total PPO minus the signal line.

The PPO is going to indicate when two averages are likely to converge or diverge. The PPO will be positive if the 12 period EMA is greater than the 26 period EMA. The greater the distance between the pair, the more positive the PPO will be. Likewise, the PPO will be negative if the 12 period EMA is lower than the 26 period EMA and the greater the difference between the pair the more negative the PPO is going to be.

When the PPO crosses the 0-line moving upward then you are going to want to buy and when it moves in the other direction you are going to want to sell. Additionally, you are going to want to buy if the PPO crosses above the signal line and sell when it crosses below it.

Finally, the PPO is useful when it comes to finding hidden divergences as they typically indicate a continuation of the current trend. A hidden bullish divergence appears when the market forms high lows and the indicator forms lower lows. A hidden bearish divergence occurs when the market forms lower highs and the indicator forms higher highs.

As an example, assume an underlying asset is in a long-term uptrend and it approaches a previously relevant resistance level like a daily, weekly, monthly or even yearly high but the PPO diverges instead of following along with the price. This indicates that a reversal or price correction is likely to occur which means you would want to sell as it is unlikely that the price will continue moving upward and break through the existing resistance level. In this case you would want to set a stop loss that is roughly 5 percent higher than the currently identified resistance level.

CHAPTER 8: STOCHASTIC OSCILLATOR STRATEGY

The stochastic oscillator is a type of momentum indicator which compares the closing price of an underlying asset to the range of prices it achieved over a specific period of time. The sensitivity of this oscillator to specific movements of the market can be reduced by adjusting the time period or through the process of taking a moving average of its results.

The stochastic oscillator was created in the 1950s by a man named George Lane. It was designed to present the location of the closing price of a stock in relation to that stock's high and low range over what is typically a 14-day period. Lane developed the oscillator in such a way that it does not follow volume, price or anything similar indicators follow. Instead, it follows the speed of the price movement. As a rule, the speed of the price movement tends to change before the price itself changes which makes it easier to use a stochastic oscillator to predict reversals before they happen based on when the indicator present bearish or bullish divergences.

The stochastic oscillator also plays an important role when it comes to determining if a specific underlying asset is oversold or overbought due to the fact that it remains range bound. Its range is between 0 and 100 and will always remain constant regardless of how quickly or slowly the underlying asset moves. The traditional setting for this oscillator is 20 as the oversold threshold with the overbought threshold appearing at 80. These levels are adjustable, however, so they can be altered to fit the characteristics of specific assets or analytical requirements. Readings that come back higher than 80 show that the security in question is trading near the top of its range and readings under 20 show that it is trading at the bottom of its range.

The stochastic oscillator can be calculated via the following formula:

- C = the most recent closing price

- L14 = the low of the 14 previous trading sessions

- H14 = the highest price traded during the same 14-day period

- Percent K= the current market rate for the currency pair

- Percent D = 3-period moving average of Percent K

The idea here is that if a market is trending upward then the prices will close nearer to a high and if the market is trending downward then the prices will close near the low. With this in mind, then transaction signals are formed when the Percent K crosses through 3-period moving average, otherwise known as the Percent D.

The most important trading signal that is created by the stochastic oscillator is the divergence between the Percent D line and the price movement when the Percent D line is either oversold or overbought. This occurs when the price reaches a new bottom or top and the Percent D line fails to do the same. When prices reach a double top the stochastic oscillator's value tends to be significantly decreased during the period of the second top's development. This is considered a type of bearish divergence which means it can be used to know when to buy into falling prices.

However, many traders prefer to wait until the Percent K line crosses the Percent D line before making their first move as this tends to help the oscillator generate signals that are more refined. Both techniques are equally valid, choosing the right one for you is generally a matter of the way in which you plan to trade the signal. Trading the divergence tends to require options that include a longer expiration time when compared to the time frame of the price chart you are using. On the other hand, if you plan on waiting for the Percent D line to cross the Percent K line then you will want to trade via a shorter expiration time.

Broadly, stochastic oscillator strategies work by deploying the stochastic oscillator on trading charts that focus on the daily time frame or higher as they tend to produce higher quality stochastics overall. You will want to use parameter settings of 14, 3 and 3. You will want to execute a call option whenever you find a faster moving stochastic that rises above the slower moving one and open a put option when the faster moving line drops below the slower one.

This is a very simple strategy to implement and the stochastic oscillator is a good tool when it comes to identifying quality entry points for new options. It is important to keep in mind that, as this is a lagging indicator, the alerts that it produces will sometimes not pop until the market conditions have already changed. Additionally, it can create signals that can be misleading for novice traders.

Other stochastic oscillator issues include the fact that the price can sometimes quickly progress in its original direction despite the fact that the oscillator has indicated a crossover. This can occur when the market moves too quickly for the indicator to keep up. Also, binary options identified for trade via this indicator can sometimes become susceptible to extreme price surges such as spikes, and this issue becomes more prevalent the longer you hold onto them. If you notice these sorts of market conditions then this strategy can have a difficult time responding to the changing stimuli which can make it difficult to take corrective action when needed.

Basic stochastic oscillator strategy

This strategy uses an expiration time frame of 1 hour and focuses on forex assets. When setting up this strategy it is important to track price movements in 5-minue intervals in order to ensure that you can find the entry points you are looking for.

To start, you are going to want to find an asset that is trading within a range that is well-defined which is denoted by a strong ceiling and floor. You will then want to add the stochastic oscillator to the 5-minute chart. You will then wait until the stochastic lines drop either below 20 or above 80.

Once you have found the right overbought or oversold status you will then need to wait until both lines have bounced back from the extremes. When you see these movements, you are going to want to execute the relevant option based on the direction of the retraction and set a 1-hour expiration period.

It is important to only use this strategy with assets that are currently trading in range. You can use it with options that are trending but you will need to only open binary options in the direction the primary price movement is moving in if you do so. Be patient and never let your need to trade force you into premature trades that could cost you serious losses.

15-minute stochastic oscillator strategy

For this strategy, you are going to use a combination of technical indicators including a pair of EMAs, the RSI and the stochastic oscillator. You will need a short-term 5-day EMA and a 10-day EMA as well. You will use the default RSI setting and a slow stochastic with settings of 5, 3 and 3 with standard overbought and oversold margins. The time frame for this strategy is 15 minutes with the expiration at 60 minutes.

Call entries: In order to place a call, you are going to need the 5-day EMA to cross the 10-day EMA moving upwards. The RSI will need to be between 50 and 70. The slow stochastic will need to be between 20 and 80 and on the rise.

Put entries: If you are placing a put then the 5-day EMA will need to cross the 10-day EMA in a downward fashion. The RSI will need to stand between 30 and 50. The slow stochastic will need to be moving downward but still in between 20 and 80.

It is important for all 3 conditions to be met in order for this strategy to be successful. You will want to set your expiration point at 1-hour and let the option play out completely in order to see the best results.

CONCLUSION

Thank you for making it through to the end of *Binary Options: Strategies on How to Excel Trading Binary Options*, let's hope it was informative and able to provide you with all of the tools you need to achieve your goals, whatever it is that they may be. Just because you've finished this book doesn't mean there is nothing left to learn on the topic, expanding your horizons is the only way to find the mastery you seek. New binary options trading strategies are always being developed and not keeping up with the latest trends is a good way to find yourself outclassed by more studious traders. Don't put your trading capital at risk, continue to do your homework.

When it comes to protecting your trading capital it is equally important to practice before committing yourself to a new strategy that may, or may not, work for you in practice. Don't forget, it is best to test prospective strategies with low trade stakes as opposed to fake money as only when real money is on the line will your natural trading patterns kick in which means that something that works in a fake scenario might not be your cup of tea when it comes to trading with it in the real world. If you don't find a strategy that works for you right away, keep at it, becoming an expert binary options trader is a marathon, not a sprint, slow and steady wins the race.

Sign Up & Join <u>Andrew Johnson's Mailing List!</u>

*EXCLUSIVE UPDATES

*FREE BOOKS

*NEW REALEASE ANNOUCEMENTS BEFORE ANYONE ELSE GETS THEM

*DISCOUNTS

*GIVEAWAYS

FOR NOTIFACTIONS OF MY *NEW RELEASES* :

Never miss my next FREE PROMO, my next NEW RELEASE or a GIVEAWAY!

www.ingramcontent.com/pod-product-compliance
Lightning Source LLC
Chambersburg PA
CBHW071602210326
41597CB00019B/3371